A WINNING BUSINESS

KEN LEE

ISBN 978-1-09808-699-2 (paperback)
ISBN 978-1-09808-700-5 (digital)

Copyright © 2021 by Ken Lee

All rights reserved. No part of this publication may be reproduced, distributed, or transmitted in any form or by any means, including photocopying, recording, or other electronic or mechanical methods without the prior written permission of the publisher. For permission requests, solicit the publisher via the address below.

Christian Faith Publishing, Inc.
832 Park Avenue
Meadville, PA 16335
www.christianfaithpublishing.com

Printed in the United States of America

Contents

Preface 5
Different Breed of Cat 9
Leadership 18
Entrepreneurial Spirit 30
Manager of Business 43
The Accountants and Me 51
Modern Man, Artist, and Architecture 63
Science and Global Warming 77
Legacy of War 91

Preface

I began to reflect a situation or experience we all have in common at the young age of seven. Traumatic and torn with fear as I was at the time, fearful of any kind of recognition from friends or, rather, bullies that I knew; my two front teeth had fallen out.

Why? What was the reason for God's punishment in this manner? After all, I went to church every Sunday. I read all my devotionals. I said my prayers before I went to bed. I even obeyed the Ten Commandments.

But why? Youthful lack of understanding inspires more and more torment from the divine. Yes, I was suddenly the most disfigured human being on the planet Earth.

Our Omnipotent God, the Alpha and Omega, life and the eternal light, has a funny sense of humor. Do you not agree?

At the tender age of seven, our comprehension of the matter is drowned with fear.

What have I forgotten to do? Am I truly forgiven for my sin?

When we walk through the storms of life, often, we forget to hold our head up high. A victory has already been prepared and declared in our path and in our behalf from the moment we accept Jesus Christ.

Yes, this too shall pass with faith.

If not me, then who? If not now, then when?

Leadership is a potent combination of strategy and character. But if you must be without one, be without the strategy.
—Norman Schwarzkopf Jr.

Different Breed of Cat

On a sleepy stretch of Highway 114 just outside of Roanoke, Texas, lived a golf legend named Byron Nelson (1912–2006). John Byron Nelson was an American golf professional between 1935 and 1946. He was widely considered to be one of the greatest golfers of all time.

Nelson and two other legendary golfers, Ben Hogan and Sam Sneed, were also born within seven months after the other in 1912. Although Byron Nelson won many tournaments in his career, he is mostly recognized for winning eleven consecutive tournaments and eighteen total tournaments in 1945. Byron Nelson received the Bob Jones Award, the highest honor given by the United States Golf Association in recognition of distinguished sportsmanship in golf.

When Nelson was eleven years old, his family moved to Fort Worth, Texas, and at the age of twelve, he began caddying at Gleneagles Country Club. On his caddying, Byron Nelson said, "I knew nothing about caddying, but it was not hard to learn."

"Legendary golfer Byron Nelson, a lifelong member of Church of Christ, known as much for his gentlemanly conduct as his fifty-two PGA Tour Victories, died Tuesday at the age of ninety-four."

"We have lost a great man. Byron Nelson was a wonderful example whose life had a profound and lasting impact on everyone he met."

"Because it helps people," he said, winning the unheard-of eleven tournaments in a row.

Soon after his baptism at age twelve in the Church of Christ, Byron Nelson met Ben Hogan at the country club while caddying, and soon at a country club tournament, he beat him at age fourteen. "Winning."

With fondness, I remember many Dallas championship matches named for this legend. He would sit at the end of the tournament, perched high enough to see the players come in. The tremendous respect shown by Byron Nelson to all the players was poignant to watch. From the caring nature he took to place the pin each day to the welcome at the 18th was fun for everyone at the tournament in Dallas. Usually big names from golf, known celebrity from across the country, as well as a known personalities from the political sector were in attendance.

It was a major event in the history of Dallas with Byron in attendance, and to this day Dallas welcomes the tournament each and every year.

Being from Fort Worth, I knew a lot more about this golfing legend than most. As a very young man, I would look to the left or the right when passing by the estate just to see a glimpse of the native from Fort Worth. He was in regular attendance at a local church, and although not much was said, at certain dinners out, I could overhear their conversations. The whole town of Roanoke took great pride in their longtime resident.

Today the church stands quiet but has developed into a rather large one in Roanoke. The city of Trophy Club has today recognized the one time great, the living legend, with a high school named for him.

Time stands still, but life goes on in Roanoke, Texas.

Byron Nelson once said of playing golf, "They are a different breed of cat." Of winning, someone had to show them how so it could be enjoyed by all. As I pondered those two statements, how unlike all of us he was.

The game of golf is for the young, strong, and full of energy with a drive to be the best at a skill that is less than forgiving. From the drive of match play to the putt to sink a birdie, the skill needed to "make the shot" with precision accuracy and never overplay or outstep each play during a match makes each player one of a kind.

A WINNING BUSINESS

You hear all the comparisons "be the ball" or "be the flag." Golf is a club-and-ball sport where players use a variety of clubs to hit balls into holes on a course.

While the modern game of golf began in the fifteenth century Scotland, the game and its origins are in much debate. The Roman game of paganica; the Chinese game of chuiwan; however, the eighteenth hole at Scotland's Old Course at St Andrews in 1764, golf's first major holds promise for golf's formation.

Every round of golf is oriented in a number of holes and playing them from a teeing ground or tee box, while the initial shot on a hole is intended to move the bail forward usually 210 m and the shot is usually called a drive.

In stroke play, competitions are played in a strict rule. Each player hits his or her ball until it's holed, no matter the number of strokes. In match play, a player can pick up the bail and "surrender the hole" when it becomes mathematically impossible to win the hole. Thus, it is also acceptable to surrender the hole after playing or hitting three strokes more than par known as a triple bogey.

Penalties are incurred in certain situations. They are counted toward a player's score as if they were extra swings at the ball. Strokes are added for rule infractions or for hitting a ball into an unplayable situation.

Putting is considered to be the most important component of the game. As the game of golf has evolved, there have been many types of grips and techniques for putting.

There are two different forms of golf play: match play and stroke play. Stroke play is far more popular. The other forms of play of the game of golf are bogey competitions, skins, 9-points, Stableford, team play, and unofficial team variations.

In the world, there are 34,011 golf courses as of 2015, and the US holds the lead with 45 percent of the world's total. There are 15,372 in the United States of America, with Japan in a distant second place with 2,383.

Men's major championship game, women's major championship, and senior major championship game—each benefit the players of the chosen field.

Reflecting the status of John Byron Nelson in comparison to past national heroes and what the dimensions of attitude are for them brings "winning" in the art of excellence.

Our national heroes exhibited the same sacrifice for our country in which Byron Nelson had for the game of golf. Sometimes, we as the observers of the seen or of our national history are very similar. For circumstance may differ, and with that stated, the acceptance of the standards for sacrifice and excellence is without a doubt the same.

Every coin minted in the United States bears along with it the bust of a past hero these words LIBERTY—In God We Trust. It was not lightly that our forefathers chose these words, for they knew the tremendous cost and sacrifice that had been paid to secure our freedom. In gratitude, they continually acknowledged that God had made and preserved our nation. They were confident that God was blessing their endeavors because they acknowledged Him and sought His aid in all their doings. They warned future generations that "the day God was not earnestly revered in America, she would become a byword among nations." Our nation's founding fathers knew how to count the cost of liberty. On July 4, 1776, there was signed in the City of Philadelphia one of America's historical documents: the Declaration of Independence. It marked the birth of this nation, which under God, was destined for world leadership.

We often forget that in declaring independence from an earthly power, our forefathers made a forthright declaration of dependence upon Almighty God. The closing words of this document solemnly declare "With a firm reliance on the protection of Divine Providence, we mutually pledge to each other our Lives, our Fortunes and our sacred Honor."

The fifty-six courageous men who signed that document understood that this was not just high-sounding rhetoric. They knew that if they succeeded, the best they could expect would be years of hardship in a struggling new nation. If they lost, they would face a hangman's noose as traitors.

Whatever ideas we might have of these men who met to sign this pledge that hot summer in Philadelphia, it is important that we remember certain facts about them: they were not poor men but rather men of means. Most enjoyed much ease and luxury in their personal lives and were respected in their communities. However, they considered liberty much more important than the security they enjoyed and pledged their lives, fortunes, and their sacred honor to that end. They fulfilled their pledge, paid the price, and freedom was won.

To be born free is a privilege. To die free is an awesome responsibility and purchased at great cost.

John Adams said, "I am well aware of the Toil and Blood and Treasure, that it will cost Us to maintain this declaration, and support and defend these States.—Yet through all the Gloom I can see the Rays of ravishing Light and Glory. I can see that the End is worth all the Means."

"To those who sacrificed for our freedom, the end was worth sometimes painful means. Where would we be today if there had not been those who counted the cost for freedom and 'Willingly' paid for it? Where will we be tomorrow if men and women of integrity do not come forward today to pay the price for maintaining America's freedom?" Ben Franklin said when asked what he had given us, "A republic, if you can keep it."

So this new creation stood unique, a system of self-government by the consent of the governed. A constitutional republic with individual liberty, elected representatives, and limited government. A government with its powers nailed down, fastened, and confined to the proper defense of the individual to pursue life, liberty, and happiness. All the inalienable rights endowed by the Creator. A republic in which checks and balances were in place to stop any tyrant and protect all its citizens.

After God, the individual came first. Only by His consent could government govern, and then only to protect life, liberty and property. Not just his, but that of all men equally.

Our founding fathers realized the impossibility of maintaining freedom unless those who are "at liberty" are able to exercise self-restraint. And they gave to this government just enough power to serve its people. Just enough power and no more.

Even then, with all the checks and balances of that constitutional document, it was not until the Bill of Rights was written that the states consented to the union and ratified the federation.

The concept of a secular state was virtually nonexistent in 1776 as well as in 1787 when the Bill of Rights was adopted. "To read the Constitution as the charter for a secular state is to misread history and misread it radically. The Constitution was designed to _____ a Christian order."

Why then is there an absence of any reference to Christianity in the Constitution? Because the framers of the Constitution did not believe that this was an area of jurisdiction for the federal government. It would not have occurred to them to attempt to reestablish that which the colonist had fought against, namely religious control and establishment by the central government.

Separation of church and state? Absolutely!

Separate God from government? Not so!

The very purpose of the Pilgrims in 1620 was to establish a government based on the Bible. The New England Charter, signed by King James I, confirmed this goal: "to advance the enlargement of Christian religion, to the glory of God Almighty." "Governor Bradford, in writing of the Pilgrim's landing, describes their first act: 'Being thus arrived in a good harbor and brought safe to land, they fell upon their knees and blessed God of Heaven…'"

The fulfillment of that charter would not occur overnight or within the lifetime of any of the Pilgrims. The coming generations would require quality education to continue their quest.

Probably no segment of American education has turned out greater numbers of illustrious graduates than New England's Ivy League. Harvard, Yale, and Princeton still carry their own mystique and an aura of elitism and prestige.

Yet perhaps it would surprise most people to learn that almost every Ivy League school was established primarily to train ministers of the gospel and to evangelize the Atlantic Seaboard.

It took only eighteen years from the time the Pilgrims set foot on Plymouth Rock until the Puritans, who were among the most educated people of their day founded the first and perhaps the famous

Ivy League school, Harvard. Their Rules and Precepts adopted in 1646, included the following essentials: "Let every Student be plainly instructed, and earnestly pressed to consider well, the maine end of his life and studies is, to know God and Jesus Christ which is eternal life…"

By the turn of the century, Christians in the Connecticut region launched Yale as an alternative to Harvard. Many thought Harvard too far away and too expensive, and they also observed that the spiritual climate at Harvard was not what it once had been.

Princeton, established in 1746 retained its evangelical vigor longer than any other Ivy League school. In fact, Princeton's presidents as well as many of its faculty were evangelical until the turn of the twentieth century.

"With the exception of the University of Pennsylvania, every collegiate institution founded in the colonies prior to the Revolutionary War was established by some branch of the Christian church."

Whether you are Christian or not, consider this warning. If we abandon our Christian roots for pluralism, we will soon lose all attending benefits of a Christian civilization such as law, moral standards, limited government, and any vestige of liberty that we still maintain.

It is imperative to understand that from the beginning the Bible was the foundation for the American system of government. In fact, John Adams said, "The highest glory of the American Revolution was this: it connected in one indissoluble bond the principles of civil government with the principles of Christianity."

John Whitehead, a constitutional lawyer and historian analyzes the Supreme Court's understanding of the above truth in a recent article. "In 1892 the United States Supreme Court made an exhaustive study of the supposed connection between Christianity and the government of the United States. After researching hundreds of volumes of historical documents, the Court asserted 'these references add a volume of unofficial declarations to the mass of organic utterances that this is a religious people…a Christian nation.' Likewise in 1931, Supreme Court Justice George Sutherland reversed the 1892 decision in relation to another case and reiterated that Americans are a 'Christian people' and in 1952 Justice William O. Douglas presuppose a Supreme Being."

It is obvious from these men and declarations that the providential view of history held away over much of American life well into the nineteenth century.

In the twentieth century our educational system took on a new look called progressive education. Under this system of teaching, "humanism" took shape and gradually became the dominant ideology of the American public school system. Most Americans, including most Christians, are products of our progressive educational system. Hopeless youths drag through their civics and social studies classes deprived of the providential view under the provision of the separation of church and state. As a result of this educational tragedy, humanist views of history are all that we have been taught for generations.

Humanism is not the only attack upon our educational system and inherited ideals.

The Marxist view of history as defined by Marx in his Economics and Philosophic Manuscripts of 1844, says: "The entire so-called history of the world is nothing but the creation of man through human labour..." His anti-Christian interpretive scheme and that of his protégés has subtly permeated not only the Communist world but American culture as well. This historical materialism sees man as an economic unit caught in class struggle. This is why Marxist and socialist, when taking over a country, will purge the people of any Christian heritage and indoctrinate them with their own.

In conclusion, the following statement by the eminent professor and theologian Charles Hodge of Princeton Seminary in 1876 illustrates the cogent and balanced thinking that once prevailed concerning our nation: "The proposition that the United States of America is a Christian and Protestant nation, is not so much the assertion of a principle as the statement of fact. The fact is not simply that the great majority of the people are Christians and Protestants, but that the organic life, the institutions, laws, and official action of the government, whether that action be legislative, judicial, and executive, is, and of right should be, and in fact must be, in accordance with the principles of Protestant Christianity."

Our Christian foundations and what is left of the Godly institutions must be passed on as a legacy. Being Christian or not, we are held accountable for what we do with this unprecedented heritage. To whom is given much is required.

Leadership

Leaders must not only assess the current performance honestly and fairly but also wisely judge the potential for improvement at a pace which progress can realistically be made. Leadership depends on trust, and trust is grounded in the shared understanding of what is working in the best interest of the company and its personnel, and what is not steady job progress will improve credibility and gain favor among others in authority.

While a leader holds a position of authority, the real power to affect change resides in the subordinates who pledge their support and believe in the administrative power of the company.

By understanding the relationship that my company, Altamont Custom Homes Inc. has within the community, it has allowed me to develop the skills necessary to direct others, purchase materials, provide jobs, tax revenue, and all the other benefits a small business has on our economy. This entrepreneurship exert influence over others.

As an owner of a corporation, I find that leaders always lead by example and direct policy and serve as a guide to others' moral conduct and exemplify standards of excellence.

The desire to understand people, their attitudes, and perceptions is key in being a successful leader. Communication will increase productivity and workers' satisfaction. Also, developing learning programs within the company will help individuals deal with stress and common problems within the workplace.

Managers play a vital role in the development and sustained productivity of any successful organization. The managers organize and direct others through disciplines involving ethics, decision making, and strategic planning.

As a manager, I work to achieve a specified goal for my company. Social, cultural, economic, political, and technological changes are occurring on every level from downsizing to outsourcing. The skills I have acquired from the company I own concentrate on strategic thinking, effective communication, and the ability to foster a sense of teamwork and empowerment of my work.

The major challenges I face as a manager is developing techniques that promote better job performance in the workplace. Learning how to develop effective measures to solve problems, such as assessing customer satisfaction and employee attitudes.

Managers require the knowledge of organizational behavior to better understand the culture and diversity of culture within the workplace. Current issues commonly found in organizational settings are layoffs, extreme workloads, ineffective supervision, burnout, and health care. Managers are the catalyst creating the infrastructure for transformation within the organization.

At its best, leadership is collaborative experience of teaching and learning, and a leader who reveals all sides of the truth prepares a way for such leadership by distinguishing real success from failure, good work from bad.

By accepting a truthful assessment, real progress toward a goal is possible. Observation is a necessary tool for leaders to manage and increase productivity in the workplace and realize positive workers' satisfaction.

Establishing credibility by accomplishing goals will prove to be the most important role of a leader. These goals should be established and approached in an outline such that the first goals will result in the success of the rest.

Encouraging the workforce through team building will result in better relations throughout the company. By encouraging managers and staff to look closely at their individual job practice and consider new ways of working together and explore unfamiliar approaches to job problems, the entire company will grow and overcome problems that arise.

The study of leadership includes ourselves looking for ways to inspire others to become better leaders as well. Leaders listen attentively, ask good questions, and explain how they interpreted what they saw and heard. In time, these traits will be assumed in the others within the team-building environment as well. By talking and sharing knowledge and expertise as a leader, we are on a teaching mission to better understand ourselves and direct others in the goal-oriented mindset of leadership.

The major challenges and opportunities for managers to use leadership principles I found in an ad that read, "Wanted: A miracle worker who can do more with less, pacify rival groups, endure chronic second-guessing, tolerate low levels of support, process large volumes of paper and work double shifts seventy-five nights out of the year. He or she will have carte blanche to innovate, but cannot spend much money, replace any personnel, or upset any constituency." I feel this is the major challenge for any leader—to be able to think outside the box and have reform-minded principles and set guidelines for action that truly help them lead.

The job and principles for any leader has become increasingly complex and constrained. Leaders find themselves locked in with less room to maneuver. At the very time that proactive leadership is essential, leaders find themselves in the least favorable position to provide it. They need a new mindset and guidelines for action to break through those who are entrapped and those who want to make a difference in their job.

Dependency is created by two interrelated conditions: overload and corresponding vulnerability to packaged solutions. First, the system fosters dependency on the part of leaders. Then the role for implementing change or innovations, more often than not, consists of being on the receiving end of externally initiated changes. The constant bombardment of new tasks and the continual interruptions keep them off balance. Not only are the demands fragmented and incoherent but even good ideas have a short shelf life, as initiatives are dropped in favor of the latest policy. Overload in the form of a barrage of disjointed demands foster this dependency.

Realizing that there is no answer that will never arrive in any formal sense can be quite liberating. Instead of hoping that the latest technique will at last provide the answer, we can then approach the situation differently. Leaders for change get involved as learners in real reform situations. They craft their own theories of change, consistently testing them against new situations. They become critical consumers of management theories, able to sort out promising ideas from empty ones, becoming less vulnerable to, and less dependent on, external answers and stop looking for solutions in the wrong places.

The contributions made by major behavioral science disciplines regarding leadership deal with ethical values, compliance with legal requirements, and respect for people and their safety.

In an age of increasing global competition, human creativity, personal productivity, and social responsibility are becoming the new frontiers of competitive advantage. The three interlinked goals of economic prosperity, environmental protection, and social equality are already at the top of corporate agendas.

In this new environment of the twenty-first century, we find ourselves making business decisions that are linked to values and respect for people. This is a new business climate that recognizes long-term sustainable profitability is directly linked to acting in a socially responsible, ethical, and compassionate manner. Creating such a culture demands a radically different management approach than that practiced in the latter half of the twentieth century. It requires of the employees and creates an environment where people find meaning and passion in their work.

It is this new business climate that recognizes the long-term profitability linked to this social responsibility. This new business culture based on caring, trust, responsibility, and strategic planning has helped to define leadership today. As corporations continue to engage in socially responsible practices, these activities will strengthen corporate reputations and increase shareholder value.

Managers require a knowledge of leadership in order to better direct others and achieve desired outcomes in their corporate structure. As I formed Altamont Custom Homes Inc., I developed the skills and disciplines that are required to establish a name and good reputation as an independent home builder.

Planning, organizing, influencing, and controlling the corporation and those who are employed are part of the many responsibilities I have. These ethics are found not only in a successful corporation but in a successful society. The influence corporations have on society is far more than just employment. They direct personal income or status in the communities we live and influence a decision-making process that affects the global economy.

Through leadership, I direct the daily responsibilities of filing franchise tax reports, acquiring loans, filing financial statements, cash flow statements, and often designing plans for new residential homes. The organizational objectives in my corporation focus on time of completion, the quality of my homes, marketing, and most important, having a satisfied customer.

Management requires strategic planning to achieve certain goals set forth in a business plan. By forecasting a project on a daily, weekly, and monthly schedule, the necessary time frame for complete-influence leadership directs the policy and serves as to guide others' conduct and exemplify standards of excellence.

A contingency approach in the study of leadership is a business challenge where members of the organization develop strategies and techniques relevant to a problem. Specific action plans are developed, including background, research methodologies, data collection, and analysis. Intervention strategies will be formulated to avoid problems within the company.

Situational theories could not predict which leadership skills would be more effective in certain situations. The contingency models focused on the fit between personality characteristics, leader's behaviors, and situational variables but did not clarify which or what of these determined effective leadership.

Subsequent leadership studies differentiated effective leaders from noneffective leadership. The comparison of effective and noneffective leaders led to the identification of two dimensions, initiating structures and consideration and revealed that effective leaders were high performers in both.

A WINNING BUSINESS

The basis of all leadership is the personal grounding of the leader and the leader's deepest values and purpose. This internal grounding will inspire vision, cultivate talent, catalyze teams, align strategy, and result in positive change.

The internal grounding of a leader provides a foundation to assess and know the organizational and competitive environment. Understanding who you are and what you stand for is the basis of personal grounding.

Contextual grounding helps leaders understand their ongoing realities in the world.

In order to inspire others, the leader must set a credible and reliable example for the organization and have a direction for the organization to go.

Leaders must work to retrain talent and develop the full potential of those you lead.

The ability to catalyze teams and mobilize individuals and groups as well as design strategy to build the organization will allow the leader of the organization to meet the ongoing challenge of leadership that results in positive change.

Decision theory is a body of knowledge and related techniques designed to help the decision maker choose among a set of alternatives in light of their possible consequences. Decision theory can apply to conditions of certainty, risk, or uncertainty.

In decision under risk, each alternative will have consequences and the probability of occurrence for each consequence is known. Therefore, each alternative is associated with a probability distribution and a choice among probability distributions.

When the probability distributions are unknown, you have decision under certainty. This theory offers a rich collection of techniques and procedures to reveal preferences and introduce them into models of decision. It is not, however, concerned with defining objectives, designing the alternatives, or assigning the consequences. Decision under certainty means that each alternative leads to one, and only one consequence and a choice among alternatives is equivalent to a choice among consequences.

In a situation under certainty, the decision maker's preferences are simulated by a single-attribute or multi-attribute value function that introduces ordering on a set of consequences and is thus also ranked by alternatives. The decision maker's preferences for the mutually exclusive consequence of an alternative are described by a function that permits a calculation of the expected result for each alternative. The alternative with the greatest expectancy for success is considered most preferable.

In the case of uncertainty, decision theory offers two main approaches. The first exploits criteria of choice developed in a broader context by game theory, as for example the max–min rule, where we choose the alternative such that the worst possible consequence is better than or equal to the best possible consequence of any other alternative. The second approach is to reduce the uncertainty case to the case of risk by using subjective probabilities based on expert assessment or on analysis of previous decisions made in similar circumstances.

The dominant values in today's workforce required to be a successful leader have changed from just being business savvy and having a general knowledge of people skills to the evolutionary, social, technological, and environmental business climate of the twenty-first century.

Today, leaders must be able to create organizations that respond more quickly and innovatively to overcome operational problems. They must provide an atmosphere where individuals find meaning, connection, balance, and growth in their professional career.

We must encourage individuals to consider the internal resources in order to bring out their full potential, nurture the communities we live along with the environment and natural resources. Foster physical and psychological well-being and interact with each other in an open and trustful environment.

By promoting these competencies in individuals, we will build character and foster the ability for others to be role models. These developmental methods will assist in a personal transformation in ourselves and others.

A WINNING BUSINESS

Due to downsizing, a greater number of hours during the work week, and extreme workloads, most American workers feel unsatisfied with the job they currently have. In the 1950s, a single income would supply the needs of a family. With the passing of each decade, two-income families have become the norm. Children are placed in day care, and many American workers feel their tax dollars do not provide an adequate education for their children. As a result, private schooling and homeschooling have become more popular. Workers feel the need to be better educated and find jobs with more income to satisfy the needs of their families.

A new survey by the Conference Board reveals that workers ages forty-five to fifty-four have the lowest job satisfaction rates at 46.5 percent satisfaction. Workers with household incomes above $50,000.00 are still the happiest of the lot, but their contentment is down from 66.5 percent in 1995 to 55.1 percent currently. Some 60 percent of those employed in the Rocky Mountains region say they are happiest with their work situations, while the lowest rating at 45.6 percent are the workers in New York, New Jersey, and Pennsylvania. Less than 174 of workers are satisfied with their employer's promotion policies and bonus plans.

Many groups meet to solve problems or make decisions. Reflective thinking involves a careful systematic approach to a problem. Groups who use reflective thinking to make their decisions make use of a six-step guide called the standard agenda.

This involves problem identification, problem analysis, criteria selection, solution generation, solution evaluation, and solution implementation.

Brainstorming is another option for decision-making. When brainstorming, group members are encouraged to generate as many ideas about a particular topic as they can. For instance, group members may use brainstorming to generate as many solutions as they can in step four of the standard agenda. Group members should be encouraged to say anything that comes to mind when brainstorming. Every idea is written down and judgments about ideas and ideas are saved until later.

Nominal group techniques are group decision-making tools used when the group must rank order a set of options. In order to use the nominal group technique, group members work individually to list all alternatives to a problem. Sometimes, nominal group technique is used after a brainstorming session is held. Then ideas are ranked from lowest to highest in priority.

A final decision will be made by using a consensus where all members agree on the final decision through discussion and debate.

The group will then give their decision to their leader and focus on the task or problem to be solved.

The strengths and weaknesses of group decision-making are weighed by the overall performance of the decision makers and the results of the decisions. Many experiments have been created to decide if individuals or committees make the best decisions. The conclusion was that committees slowed down the response time to problem resolution; however, the interaction that takes place in a group improves the decision-making process, and it was better to have a consensus to a problem than for a single individual to make decisions that affect a group.

The growing popularity of teams within organizations is based upon the feedback of multiple individuals accomplishing a single task. Organizations have found high performers involve more than just individual action as organizations compete on the global markets today. Utilizing teams within the workplace is a systematic way to establish task-oriented proficiency.

By using the teamwork concept, employees learn to cooperate with each other and obtain information from coworkers. This contributes to the team's success and shares competency with others on the staff and on other teams. It sets standards and serves as a role model and influences others by example.

The nature of leadership can be developed through teaching methods and training. The goals describing the nature of leadership encompass the need for vision, understanding the difference between leadership and management, identifying a leadership style, and understanding the importance of personal and ethical behavior.

Leaders develop skills in interpersonal communication and develop skills in leading the meetings of a group. They understand the process of making a good decision and what makes a decision "good" and the steps that are necessary to make those decisions. Skills in building teams to accomplish tasks and the ability to help others develop into their full potential are also a necessary function. By accomplishing goals using orderly steps, leaders display their ability to accomplish tasks.

Fred Fielder's contingency model explains that group performance is a result of the interaction of two factors. These factors are known as leadership style and situational favorableness. Leadership style is the consistent system of interaction between a leader and a work group. An individual's leadership style depends on his or her personality and is thus fixed. The second is known as situational favorableness or environmental variable. This is the degree a situation enables a leader to exert influence over a group. I have realized the influence these have on my organizational activities and have motivated subordinates and served as a better source of communication within my corporate environment.

The path-goal theory of leadership focuses on numbers, reports, and encourages leaders and managers to look at the world primarily through relationships, fostering an atmosphere of learning and top job performance. This motivation of a group is accomplished in several ways: offering rewards for achieving performance goals, clarifying paths toward these goals, and removing obstacles to better performance. I apply these styles of leadership with directive, supportive, participative, and achievement-oriented leadership.

Situational leadership theory recognizes that traits or preferable behavior factors are not sufficient to predict leadership success and lead to the focus on situational influence. Situational models assert that no one of the leadership styles works in every situation. Most studies have identified critical situational factors that influence leadership style and effectiveness. Situational leadership provides leaders and managers with practical tools like self-assessment to help them recognize their own leadership style and identify areas for adjustment. I believe a successful leader is one who can adapt their behavior to meet the demands of their own unique situations.

Leader-member exchange theory asserts that leaders develop relationships with each member of their work group. A high-quality relationship is characterized by members having high levels of responsibility, decision influence, and access to resources. Members that enjoy a high level of leader-member exchange are said to be in the "in group." A low-quality leader-member exchange offers low levels of support to the members, and they are classified as being in the "out group." High-quality relationships bring more responsibility and higher satisfaction, while low quality relationships bring less responsibility and lower satisfaction.

The leader-participation model provides influence within the group and can lead to better understanding and cooperation. Highly structured tasks can be performed with more influence over group action. This involvement requires communication skills and disciplines for the leader or manager. A work-team goal or mission is clearly defined, and problem-solving techniques and remedies are developed within the group.

Leadership deals with the development of high-quality relationships with each member of the work group. These high-quality relationships lead to more responsibility and greater job satisfaction, promotion, productivity, and organizational commitment. Power deals with the influence a person has over others within an organization. The ability to hire of fire, discipline or reward; and this is not, however, to be confused with respect. A good leader develops and maintains relationships, and the members gain favor, respect, and trust.

Conflict in business is disruptive to the company itself. The mutual antagonism of leadership leads to the destruction of any company or business. The mutual opposition of leadership is theorized to be related to work and behavioral changes within the workplace. For example, conflict leads to outcomes such as employee loss in productivity, job dissatisfaction, withdrawal or resignation.

There are five key steps in the negotiation process. First, recognition of conflict by the parties. Identify the goals and needs, and realize exactly what you are trying to achieve. Second, the negotiation process by the parties. Decide who can help; if the conflict is resolved, stop. Third, convincing the disputants by a neutral or third party. Plan to network with both individuals and groups; remember the goals each side has to attain. Set time, place, and date for legal representation. Fourth, follow-up meeting. Develop questions from each disputant and select a new process and negotiation director. If resolved, stop. The fifth step in the negotiation process is the avoidance of the power play, or a complete breakdown in negotiations will result, and each side will go to court. Know what you can provide, and then explain the goals of each side. Show how this opportunity best prepares each party for an agreement that is mutually beneficial, and then, sign the documents.

The six key elements that define an organization's structure build the future to organizational leaders.

First, there must be a clear understanding of the business across functional areas that improve the large-scale cross-functional processes. Second, framework and tools to deliver breakthroughs in performance. Third, the exposure to current leadership in the organization must be in place. Fourth, change in management experience through leading organizations through rapid change within the organization itself. Fifth, confidence in the driving force behind the business results. Finally, mentoring and a stable coaching network that identifies problems within the organization and develops new skills for overcoming the problems in the organization.

By defining key elements of an organization's structure, programs can be developed to groom future organizational leaders to improve the organization itself.

Many initiatives that have been historically implemented have some value as a result of improper implementation. Without time to actually drive process improvements, these results will be meager.

Entrepreneurial Spirit

The entrepreneur has become the cornerstone of the American capitalistic society. The United States Office of Advocacy analysis of small business in 1999 estimated the United States had approximately 5.8 million businesses with employees of which 99.7 percent were businesses with less than five hundred employees.

To understand the entrepreneur, you must examine the individual business. Ask how and where your customers will get your products and services. Understand what kind of business you will have: wholesale, retail, or service. Will you sell on the internet or use supplementary sales channels? Sell by mail order or in-person sales calls? Will you have a sales staff, and will it be in-house or outsource marketing? Will you use independent wholesalers, distributors, sales representatives, or sale through your own store or office? All these criteria help us to understand the role of today's entrepreneur.

By any measure, the small business is critical to the economic well-being of this country. Recent figures indicate 52 percent of the total private sector, non-farm employees were small businesses with fewer than five hundred employees.

Small businesses were concentrated in the sectors which include construction, agriculture services, and wholesale trades. These trades create new businesses and jobs. They help to create innovative services and products which are sold at the marketplace. They provide business ownership opportunities to a diverse and traditionally underrepresented group, which now pays taxes and contributes to the well-being of the economy as a whole.

These contributions are clearly established in the US Small Business Administration's Office of Advocacy.

Women-owned business in 1999 represented 37 percent of the total self-employed nationwide.

Minority-owned business, according to the latest figures compiled by the census bureau in 1992, show there were nearly two million minority-owned businesses. This includes roughly 630,000 Black-owned businesses; 780,000 Hispanic-owned firms; 606,000 films owned by Asians, Pacific Islanders, American Indians, and Alaskan Natives.

In almost all industries, the most prolific job creators were firms with fewer than five employees in the United States.

The manager or owner of a small business must be able to find his or her niche in society. To develop this further, you must understand how your business will deliver your product to your consumer and understand who your customer is anyway. If you will be selling through retail stores, for example, the store owner or decision maker will be your customer. Understanding the customer can increase your sales significantly and have a strong impact on the product line itself.

How your business begins to develop will lead to decisions on a sales staff. Additional help may be necessary to actually grow the business. The best time to understand how you will handle the issue of sales management and compensation for a staff is before additional staff is hired.

If you purchase raw materials or products, you must consider shipping costs. These costs will have an effect on the profit or return on investment. If costs push you to a level where you cannot make an appropriate return, new ways of shipping or an adjustment in the price may be necessary.

Advertising in today's marketplace is essential. Print advertising, such as local newspapers, is probably the most widely used form of advertising. These ads target a general population, usually within the area of your business's most likely sales.

Trade publications are considered useful tools because industries group their products and services and have specific methods of reaching new markets. These also list the newest products and services and combine many companies so that exposure to the industry is expanded.

Media advertising on the radio or television is not generally considered to be the most cost-effective way to promote a business. However, the number of possible consumers exposed to the product or business is very large. This exposure can be very beneficial especially if this method is used repeatedly and the target population soon remembers the advertising and business.

Radio and television advertising are also sold at more competitive prices during what is considered to be "off hours."

Outdoor billboard advertising and yellow pages advertising are also widely use strategies to promote companies, services, and reach large sections of the local population.

Developing marketing strategies through different promotions, publicity, tradeshows, and even word-of-mouth referrals will bring repeat business and success to the company.

As I formed Altamont Custom Homes Inc., I understood the role of the small businessman. As with most small businesses, I did most everything relating to the management myself. Everything from cleaning the office to the design of the custom homes, and even the sales. If you are a small business with no great expansion plans, you may remain your own best, and perhaps only sales representative.

Being the manager and owner, I focused on the critical interpersonal relationships and sought ways to better understand and influence the people I employed and the other organizations I dealt with daily. My role was to organize and direct others as I sought out disciplines such as ethics, strategic planning, and communication between the workforces. Having preestablished goals is the integral part of this communication and conformity within my company.

Employees within the workplace expect compensation for productivity and training strategies to promote their job performance and better resolve conflicts through team building and internal relationships. By understanding my role as a manager, I am able to cope and better understand the stress-related behaviors of the individual employee and design strategies for managing individual crises.

A WINNING BUSINESS

By understanding the relationship my company has within the community, this allows me to better understand my abilities as an entrepreneur. This relationship of fulfilling a need for new residences within the marketplace allows my company to grow, provide jobs, tax revenue, and all the other benefits a small business has on our economy. With the understanding of my important role in purchasing raw materials for the construction of new homes, organizing a labor force, constructing new homes, and making a profit, I have displayed the leadership and entrepreneurial principles that is necessary for a healthy society.

I evaluate and make changes to my company based on a year-to-year analysis of the quality of my products and the profits of my company. By understanding these relationships, I can modify the product to meet expectations for the next year. By using this forecasting method, projects can be planned in advance on a weekly, monthly, or yearly schedule. This develops a time frame for project completion and allows me to predict the best course of action for my company.

The fundamentals and basic principles of my organization are found mostly in my ability to keep up with the necessary paperwork and the systematic combination of workforce required to bring a project to its completion.

The need to understand people, then attitudes, and perceptions are key in being a successful manager. Communication between the management and employees will increase productivity and worker's satisfaction. Also, developing learning programs within the company will help individuals deal with stress and common problems within the workplace.

I have learned that control over the employees has a lot to do with compromise. As a manager, I can best perform this role and delegate this this authority to my employees through the mediation process. By using this control, everyone under the manager's authority contributes to a better understanding of the goals and desires of the company as a whole.

There are many effective marketing tools and services that will expand and promote a company. The most commonly used is advertising in the newspaper. This is the most affordable and simplest form of marketing. Two line ads to full-page color ads can be run weekly and reach a wide population.

Many companies will use graphic design artist to help with printed materials that will be mass-mailed to a specific list of people. Mass-mail media marketing firms promote products, goods, and services to a specific group and by targeting this way, the company will have better results.

Internet marketing has become the latest way to promote goods and services. Internet markets and corn companies have changed the way people around the world do business. No longer do consumers have to drive to a store to shop. With a simple click of a mouse and fast delivery of any product, time and money are saved for the consumer, most of whom work forty to sixty hours a week. This has also made home business possible without having to keep a large sales staff or in-house inventory. Many new businesses today are being started by stay-at-home housewives who successfully market goods and services to supplement their household incomes.

Websites are the means companies use to promote goods and services. These sites are inexpensive, and consumers from around the world can "log on" and view companies and products of all kinds. This has also created a new market along with new jobs. Professional website designers have become highly demanded and are necessary for many companies to get started in this internet business.

E-mail promotions are sent out every day to millions of people and have brought people from thousands of miles apart together. E-mail directories are sold to companies and are used for mass marketing. Many are just informational and useful to the individual, but most are unsolicited or "spam." Removing your e-mail address can be a complicated process and is very time consuming for the individual.

Promotional products might be given away at trade shows where you will find a large gathering of people from one specific industry. These trade show events are usually held in large public forums and tickets are sold to cover the cost of the event. These trade shows are publicized and bring in revenue for both the sponsor and the city holding the event. Every type of industry is represented at some time during the year, making this a great way to gain exposure for your company.

Up to the minute news letters can be sent out on a schedule to inform people of new products and differences, separating your company from others. These letters help bring a sense of unity to the group and can state everything from company goals to stock prices. This information can be a very useful tool in keeping and growing a company.

These tools are used daily by small business and large corporations. Every business needs some form of marketing to establish itself in the marketplace and differentiate itself from other companies.

Financial planning is the key to success for the individual, small business, and large corporation. Most businesses and individuals today rely on bank finance for capitalization and investment purposes to grow their business. However, this is just a part of financial planning and a successful strategy for company growth, college tuition, personal wealth accumulation, and retirement.

If you work for a small business or a large corporation, a 401k account is very familiar. This is an account in which a portion of the monthly net proceeds is deposited into an account and the dollar amount is matched (some by a percentage) by the small business or corporation. This money can be used for retirement or creatively moved to other investments. This is a sure and reliable way to save money with little risk.

Having children today requires a special college fund to be started before they reach kindergarten. This will allow the parents enough time to save what is estimated to be in for year 2014, for a sum of $400,000.00 for a private college education. This education will be necessary to ensure for future employment of the child in a competitive marketplace and the success of the entire family unit itself. There are many growth funds available that allow parents to save and place their children into a degreed program that will allow them to compete in the ever competitive job market of the twenty-first century.

Estate planning is usually done with the consultation of a professional estate planner. The goal is to grow foe individual's estate through strategies such as real estate investment, tax incentives, and charitable contributions to minimize the yearly consumption of capital. Revenues from stocks, annuities, and other investments are a part of the process of estate planning. There are many tax-free growth funds that have no risk and a good rate of return. These funds are considered to be an integral part of a safe retirement when compared to just investing in the stock market.

Having a CPA or good tax consultant is necessary to protect as much revenue as possible from yearly tax payments. The yearly process of paying taxes is required, and every individual, small business, and corporation should have an accountant and a licensed tax consultant. This will ensure the proper return will be filled without any mistakes.

Capitalization to start a new venture is gained through either bank finance or private venture capitalization. The ability to attract new investors depends on a good reputation, good business plan, a good product or service, and a promotion that will attract the right kind of investors.

Pro forma income statements are similar to historical income statements, except it projects the future rather than tracks the past. Pro forma income statements are an important tool for planning future business operations.

Pro forma balance sheets are similar to a historical balance sheet, but it represents a future projection. Pro forma balance sheets are used to project how the business will be managing its assets in the future.

Pro forma cash flow, not profits, is the lifeblood of your business. Project it, monitor it, and manage it well before a crisis inside the company begins. These projections are very important in the decision-making process of job increases or job losses in a company.

There are many guides to successful personal finance, including budgeting, investing, saving, spending credit and debt, retirement, and much more. Financial training books, audio tapes, financial video training, and financial planning tools are all necessary tools for up-to-date individuals and businesses to plan their financial future. Many of these tools can be found on the internet and purchased or even downloaded for free. Utilization of up-to-date financial programs is necessary for individuals and companies to successfully plan their financial fixture.

As an owner and manager of a small business, I organize and direct others through disciplines involving ethics, decision-making, and strategic planning. It requires the knowledge of organizational behavior to better understand the culture and diversity of culture within the workplace.

The contingency approach is a business challenge where members of the organization develop plans to analyze strategies and techniques relevant to a problem. Specific action plans are developed, including background, research, methodologies, data collection, and analysis. Intervention strategies will be formulated to avoid problems within the company.

There are four entrepreneurial management styles that effect decision-making within an organization. The group model, which is defined as a process of arriving at a judgment as based upon the input of multiple individuals. The rational model, which is based on economic views and is grounded in goals, objectives, alternatives, consequences, and optimality. The political model, considers preconceived notions that decision makers bring to the table are motivated by their own needs. Finally, the process model, which is more structured. This model is based on standard operating procedures or preestablished guidelines within an organization.

I have found the strengths of group decisions, as an entrepreneurial style, bring feelings of inclusion within the organization. Group decisions have better defined goals for the organization and create a better environment for the employees. However, some of the weaknesses to be found is that the company may have profound changes within its structure and standard management practices. Perhaps a combination of both brings the necessary skills of strategic thinking, effective communication, and the ability to foster a sense of teamwork and empowerment to the organization.

Group decision-making is the process of arriving at a judgment based on the feedback of multiple individuals and has influence over key components of the functioning organization.

The contingency model explains that group performance is a result of the interaction of two factors. These factors are known as leadership style and situational favorableness. Leadership style is the consistent system of interaction between a leader and a work group, and individual's leadership style depends on his or her personality and is thus fixed.

Situational favorableness or the environmental variable is the degree a situation enables a leader to exert influence over a group. I have realized the influence these have on my organizational activities and have motivated subordinates and served as a better source of communication within my corporate environment.

The path-goal management style focuses on numbers, reports, and offers rewards for achieving performance goals, fostering an atmosphere of learning and top job performance.

Situational leadership provides entrepreneurs with practical tools like self-assessment, to help them recognize their own leadership style and identify areas for adjustment.

All these techniques for entrepreneurial management help develop skills that are necessary for the entrepreneur to analyze the risk and form a strategy for a successful business.

Every organization is in the business of placing capital at risk in pursuit of ventures which are uncertain. They all have goals, and they allocate resources to pursue them. Because all organizations face uncertainty in achieving their goals, they all face risk.

Enterprise risk management is about optimizing the process with which risks are taken. Recently, with perhaps the largest bankruptcy in history, the Enron company suffered staggering losses that were covered up by faulty accounting practices.

The problem is not with the financial tools but with the people who use them. While many financial tools are new, the problem of people acting fraudulently or just irresponsibly has always existed. Through appropriate oversight, corporations can act responsibly.

Through enterprise risk management, regulators are motivated to change the process corporate America does business. They seek comprehensive solutions, not because the problem is new, but because the consequences of failure have become enormous.

A WINNING BUSINESS

Implementing an effective strategy of enterprise risk management is not easy, and for each organization, it is different. There are, however, three fundamental elements which should comprise any risk strategy: corporate culture, procedures, and technology. The importance of each will vary depending upon the needs of an organization. Each will, however, be important in some sense or another.

The goal of any corporation is growth with applied ethics. This combination develops successful companies with satisfied employees. By developing high-quality relationships with each member of the work group and having clearly defined goals, remedies to problems, job satisfaction, and higher productivity will result.

By strengthening the company officers and company board, with the introduction of an in-house company structure, goals and objectives are clearly defined and corporate objectives are more easily attained. A system of company officers will be introduced to create an independent business structure. Additionally, corporate decision-making will rest with a company board system to be established in preparation for independent management of the new in-house companies.

Considerable authority invested in the company officers will be appropriate incentives based on criteria and evaluation by the business results they achieve.

Successful organizations adapt to their environment. They do so by monitoring technological, competitive, legislative, or other changes that affect their strategies and competencies. In turn, needed organizational competencies are strengthened, acquired, or if time permits, develop internally. The firm's competencies are then blended into a revised strategy which will exploit opportunities or defend against the threats found in the environment. Finally, the firm's structure is redesigned, if needed, to better support its strategy. The theory is that form or structure should follow strategy.

With this structure-driven strategy, organizations clearly write and involved in overseas communications and transportation require international distributors to act more independently than their domestic counterparts.

Establish a basis for profitability in order to grow. The firm that acts more independently from overseas inquiry leaves the element of success to chance.

Devote continuing attention to export business when the US market booms. Too many companies turn to exporting when business falls off in the United States. When domestic business starts to boom again, they neglect their export trade as if it were a secondary market.

Treat international distributors on an equal basis with domestic counterparts. Companies often carry out institutional advertising campaigns and special discount offers and so on in their United States markets but fail to make similar offers to the international distributors.

Do not assume that given market techniques and products will automatically be successful in all countries. What works in Japan may fail in Saudi Arabia. Each market has to be treated separately to ensure maximum success.

Be willing to modify products to meet regulations or cultural preferences of other countries. Local safety and security codes as well as import restrictions cannot be ignored by foreign distributors.

Print service, sale, and warranty messages in locally understood language communicate their goals and objectives. This inward view of the company asks how it will best improve the function of its productivity and quality.

Promotional aids like television, radio, newspaper, billboards, and the internet are effective tools in reaching people and building a strong, profitable, customer base for any business. By identifying clusters of customers, a company can decide how best to display your company's products and services. By understanding your strengths and weaknesses, you can capitalize on your key strengths. By understanding the customer clusters, a company can focus on the high-performance areas that represent the most profitability for the investment.

Promotional aids are the key to building a strong successful customer base. No matter the industry, telecommunications, health care, manufacturing, broadcasting, finance, retail, entertainment, services, travel, education, and yes, even government, it is clear main street marketing strategies and intelligent use of data is driving the decision-making processes of the winning players.

A basic guide to exporting is designed to help United States' firm learn the costs and risks associated with the exporting and develop a strategy for exporting. I will discuss ten keys to export success and ways to avoid the pitfalls and roadblocks that companies may encounter.

The United States GNP accounts for an excess of 84 percent generated through exporting alone. The US Department of Commerce estimates that for every $45,000.00 in export sales, one new job in the United States is created. This is more than double the amount of jobs created by domestic sales alone.

The international market is more than four times larger than the US market, and growth rates in many overseas markets far outpace the domestic market growth. By meeting and beating innovative competitors abroad, US companies can keep the edge they need at home.

There are real costs and risks associated with exporting and international trade regulations. It is therefore up to each individual company to weigh the commitments against the potential benefit.

Companies must obtain qualified export counseling and develop a master international marketing strategy before clearly define goals, objectives, and problems may be encountered.

Although the early delays and cost exporting may seem difficult to overcome compared to domestic sales, the exporter should recognize the long-range view of the process, and carefully monitor the international marketing efforts.

Take sufficient care in selecting overseas distributors (the complications in languages). Although a distributor's top management may speak English, it is unlikely that all sales and service personnel have this capability.

The last key to a successful international export business is providing readily available servicing for the product. A product without the necessary service support can acquire a bad reputation quickly.

These keys to understanding the modem entrepreneur have led to success in my personal business. I have learned many tools that have helped me to be an ethical, more positive influence on the employees and change their lives for the better. They understand the role I play in developing character and have become better individuals for the exposure to my skills as a manager. This relationship has a positive effect on the people, community, and government through the employment my company represents.

Manager of Business

The manager has always played a vital role in the development and sustained productivity of any successful organization. But as many managers are discovering, standard management practices of the past are fast becoming obsolete as organizations enter the twenty-first century.

Organizational behavior is a highly selective study designed especially for managers seeking to better understand and influence the way in which people work within their organizations. It offers an exciting alternative to traditional graduate business programs, focusing on the development of the critical interpersonal, leadership, and team building skills needed for success.

The managers organize and direct others through disciplines involving ethics, decision-making, and strategic planning. As a manager, I work to achieve a specified goal for the company. Social, cultural, economic, political, and technological changes are occurring on every level from downsizing to outsourcing. The skills I have acquired from the company I own concentrate on strategic thinking, effective communication, and the ability to foster a sense of teamwork and empowerment to my work.

The value of the systematic study of organizational behavior brings consideration to psychology to improve performance in the workplace, assessment in decision-making techniques in job performance and promotion, the climate and culture of the organization, behavioral research of employees, developing personal skills, predicting and managing individual behavior, team building, developing corporate communication, and crisis management. The major challenges I face as a manager is developing techniques that promote better job performance in the workplace, learning how to develop effective measures to solve problems, such as assessing customer satisfaction and employee attitudes. The concepts of organizational behavior bring opportunities to better understand relationships within the workplace and the expectations the consumer has of my company.

Behavioral research that is applied to organizational behavior acquaints participants with the basic premises of scientific investigation, the major methods of conducting psychological research, and the statistical procedures in analyzing data. Participants will be able to read, understand, and evaluate the research commonly used in the workplace as well as become familiar with the process of designing questionnaires and surveys, conducting field research, and using interviewing procedures.

Managers require the knowledge of organizational behavior to better understand the culture and the diversity of culture within the workplace. Current issues commonly found in organizational settings are layoffs, extreme workloads, ineffective supervision, burnout, and health care. Managers are the catalyst, creating the infrastructure for transformation within the organization.

A contingency approach is a business challenge where members of the organization develop plans to analyze strategies and techniques relevant to a problem. Specific action plans are developed, including background, research methodologies, data collection, and analysis. Intervention strategies will be formulated to avoid problems within the company.

There are three levels of analysis in the organizational behavior model. The first is designed to develop theories and methods for better analysis of an organization. Second, to integrate the material and connections and create new knowledge. Third, to understand the theory in the field can be applied in different national contexts. Theories and methods seemingly appropriate in one culture may not be universal.

There are four styles of decision-making within an organization. The group model is defined as the process of arriving at a judgment based upon the input of multiple individuals. The decisions range from small- to large-scale in scope. The rational model is based on economic view of decision-making. It is grounded in goals, objectives, alternatives, consequences, and optimality. The model assumes complete information regarding the decision to be made is available, and one correct conception of a problem can be determined. The political model considers preconceived notions that decision makers bring to the table and are motivated to act on their own needs. The process model is more structured. This model is based on standard operating procedures or preestablished guidelines within an organization. The fourth model is the garbage can model. This model is most appropriate for judgment tasks in organizations where technologies are not clear or well-defined. Many types of problems are dropped independently of each other by decision makers as these problems and solutions are generated. Not all decisions are made in a logical, political, or even standard fashion.

The dominant values in today's workforce deal with effective measures to develop their own ethics, performance, diversity, and training for promotion. Today's worker expects compensation for productivity and training strategies to promote job satisfaction and resolve conflicts by building effective teams, establishing internal relationships that effect organizational change that allows stress-related behaviors to be coped with or better strategies for managing individual crises.

Due to downsizing, a greater number of hours during the work week, and extreme workloads most American workers feel unsatisfied with the job they currently have. In the 1950s, a single income would supply the needs of a family. With the passing of each decade, two-income families have become the norm. Children are placed in day care, and many American workers feel their tax dollars do not provide an adequate education for their children. As a result, private schooling and homeschooling have become more popular. Workers feel the need to be better educated and find jobs with more income to satisfy the needs of their families.

Abraham Maslow, a member of psychologists and sociologists of the Chicago dynasty in 1943, had a great insight to the hierarchy of motivation. Self-actualization, as he called it, is the highest drive, but before a person can turn to it he or she must satisfy other lower motivations like hunger, safety, and belonging. The hierarchy has five levels. Physiological, which includes hunger, thirst, shelter, and sex. Safety, which includes security, protection from physical and emotional harm. Social, which includes affection, belonging, acceptance, and friendship. Esteem, which includes self-respect, autonomy, achievement, and status. The fifth is self-actualization or doing things. Maslow points out that the hierarchy is always shifting and does not exist by itself but is affected by the situation and general culture. Satisfaction is relative.

Douglas McGregor defined assumptions that he felt undermined the practices and stances of managers in relation to employees. These were evident from their conversations and actions. Two sets of propositions were dubbed Theory X and Theory Y. Theory X became the bad stereotype, and Theory Y the good. Theory X managers tend to believe the staff, if they had a choice, would not want to commit themselves to work for the employer. They resort to more oversight and punishment. Theory Y managers tend to believe given the right conditions for employees, their application of physical and mental effort in work is as natural as rest or play and offers satisfaction. Rewards for achievement are also associated with this manager.

The relationships I apply in business that deal with the expectancy theory are an individual act in a certain way based on the expectation that the act will be followed by a given outcome and on the attractiveness of that outcome to the individual. Effort and performance has a reward linkage that is attractive to the employee.

Group behavior is found within every organization. Informal groups formulate and implicate code of ethics or an unspoken set of standards establishing acceptable behavior, sometimes below the norm set by the organization. If the management prescribes production norms that the group considers unfair, for instance, the group's recourse is to adopt less demanding norms and to use its ingenuity to discover ways it can sabotage management's imposed standards. From the perspective of the formal group, norms generally fall into three categories: positive, negative, and neutral. In other words, norms in group behavior either support, obstruct, or have no effect on the aims of the larger organization.

Some of the strengths of group decision-making are the feeling of inclusion within the organization, better defined goals for the organization, and a better environment that serves human needs. Some weaknesses are that the organization may find profound changes to their own structure and standard management practice. Perhaps a combination of both bring the necessary skills of strategic thinking, effective communication, and the ability to foster a sense of teamwork and empowerment to the organization.

The growing popularity of teams within organizations is based upon the feedback of multiple individuals accomplishing a single task. Organizations have found high performance involves more than just individual action as organizations compete on the global markets of today. Utilizing teams within the workplace is a systematic way to establish task-oriented proficiency.

Group decision-making is the process of arriving at a judgment based on the feedback of multiple individuals and has influence over the key components of the functioning organization.

Communication is defined as the transmission of ideas and information from speeches to documents. The communication process and application to the workplace are developed in oral and written communications as well as methods for developing and disseminating corporate and work-team goals and missions. Communication takes place in all areas of the workplace, from management to employees and groups within the organization.

Some of the barriers to effective communication are a lack of clear focus on understanding the goals and objectives of the company. Sometimes it's the management's lack of understanding for the best individual hired to perform a task. Decision-making can therefore be unstructured and operating standards or preestablished goals are not met. Conformity is an integral part of the process in communication, from operations to management to employees. All must recognize the benefits of progressive communication in all areas.

Advances in technology have made companies more efficient, and information can flow faster than ever before. The computer has connected everyone within the office. And e-mail, video conference, and the internet have combined to enhance the flow of information. Executives can pass down information throughout the company in a matter of minutes. I use these technologies on a daily basis, from memos to writing cheeks to e-mail.

The undue extension of bureaus or layering of agencies that tend to oversee each other lead to a rigid adherence to administrative routine which is expensive, and the paperwork is often extreme. This system is most often found in government agencies, where money spent is often overlooked. The need for checks and balances precedes the necessity outcome of the overall good of the system itself. These agencies are run by individuals who narrowly adhere to a rigid routine, and often, efficiency is not the ultimate goal. According to Max Weber, modern bureau's function according to six principles: fixed and official jurisdictional areas, which are ordered by rules; hierarchy and levels of graded authority, where lower offices are supervised by higher ones; management is based on documents and files; officials have expert training—it requires full-time work of the official—and management follows rules.

Employees in a matrix organization spend much of their time working for other people in other organizations. Reviewing a matrix employee involves the manager of the matrix employee talking and evaluating the performance with every employee that he or she has worked with since the last review. This is a key role for the employee because he or she doesn't have just one boss but expectations of two. There are both vertical and horizontal leaders that have expectations of the job performance. In my job, I experience subcontracting, which is similar, in that I work with one individual who may use several others to actually perform the task; I hold the manager responsible for the work that is being performed. This is the same management you find in a matrix organization.

A "virtual organization" is designed to provide a service via the internet. Thousands of .com companies were created in just past few years. However, few have found a "niche" in society, and most are no longer in existence. The virtual concept for business has led to many advances in technology and has made doing business in the twenty-first century quick, simple, and fast. With internet partners worldwide, a "virtual organization" is now possible. Through the wireless office and small business web design, companies of all sizes can have exposure and offer services once only dreamed of. With the internet, companies can combine partnerships and compete on a global scale with precision, speed, and a great deal more to offer their customer.

Managers want to create organizations without boundaries by using modem technology like the internet, telecommuting, and web conferencing to grow their own organization. Through the use of these modem business tools, organizations can be brought together from around the globe. "Virtual" networking brings today's companies together no matter the distance. With little expense, a manager can create a network of companies that are woven together by using the internet and its conferencing tools.

Reengineering or a change in employee exercises from one task or skill to another has become a part of business in the twenty-first century. An effective manager has a plan for reorganization and tools for assessing the performance levels of each employee. These activities for building organizational support will develop reengineering teams that may have executive sponsors, consultants, and a staff monitoring progression. Financial justifications for capital expenditures are usually justified and an organization readiness for change also offers a good return on investment. The alternative is layoffs or job displacement.

In the workforce, there are many affected by worker obsolescence. Downsizing has led to a decline in employment in North America in just the past year. So companies are affected because of job loss and worker compensation. The employee is affected because the paycheck is reduced. This leads to less spending, which makes companies more willing to reduce profits just to stay in business, which leads to more cutbacks. The cycle of employment affects every global market around the world today. The obsolescence is not in workforce, but the skill the workforce has. Today, we find many workers who are underemployed or underpaid, who will chose to train for better future. In the building industry, many people choose to train for job advancement or career enlightenment; this adds to their value as a member of this industry.

The benefits a job has is known as job enrichment. Standard pay increases, deposits into 401k retirement plans, health care benefits, all are descriptive enrichment plans most companies have in place to keep their employees happy. There are other ways some of today's large corporations look to improve the quality of life for their employees. Internal child day care, rest periods between certain bouts of the day, the separate smoking and nonsmoking areas, all combine for a better workplace and an environment that is enriched by the employer.

Today, many workers are allowed to stay at home with the advancement of telecommuting between the home and workplace. Some of the obvious benefits are less time commuting between home and work, more time with children at home, and a set schedule with hours that can be more flexible. Some of the drawbacks are all too often more hours are actually put in at home than in a work environment, the lack of support from people within the organization itself, and interruptions that lead to late-night work. Employees probably enjoy an environment that lessens the pressure of a daily nine-to-five job and would allow for as much telecommuting as the job itself allows. The job requirements and management would have to determine this.

Being the manager and owner, I focused on the critical interpersonal relationships and sought ways to better understand and influence the people I employed in areas such as economic, psychological, or political. Transactional leadership occurs when people engage in such a way that leaders and followers raise one another to a higher moral plane.

Transactional leadership is the display of leadership that brings about the results of change within the organization. Transformational leadership is the result of these steps taken to change the environment to allow the change to take place.

In conclusion, the company I have owned and directed for the past eighteen years has led me to better understand the importance of leadership and the qualities a person has to have to lead and direct others in a way of the corporate world. Effective leadership in any organization is critical and the key to success in business itself.

The Accountants and Me

Accounting is the activity which provides quantitative information, primarily financial in nature, to assist an entity in making economic decisions. The process requires an accounting system. All information related to this activity are accounting records. An entity can be an individual or a business.

A bookkeeper is primarily responsible for the recording of business transactions and should be capable of developing and maintaining transactions as an accounting system from the gathering of documents through the production of accurate reports. A bookkeeper may have gained his or her knowledge through application or training.

An accountant is an individual who holds a degree in accounting and whose knowledge further includes the ability to analyze financial records, budget, audit, prepare tax returns, and offer management advice. An accountant may or may not also be a CPA.

A CPA is an accountant who has met the requirements for the Certified Public Accountant license or certificate. This license requires the accountant to pass a three-day examination on accounting theory, accounting practice, auditing, and business law. The examination is prepared by the American Institute of Certified Public Accountants. Individuals may seek advice of financial consultants for their personal finances. Those who do not completely understand the tax laws that affect them should rely on the services of a CPA for personal tax return preparation. Small businesses may contract the services of a respected bookkeeper and a public accounting firm whose principles are CPAs. The bookkeeper will manage daily transactions and records, while the CPA handles yearly auditing and tax preparation services along with advice when needed. A medium-sized business may employ a full-time bookkeeper. Large corporations employ CPAs and would have many bookkeepers and accounting clerks to manage their financial records.

The process of accounting is governed by a set of principles and concepts set forth by interested organizations, associations, and government bodies. These principles of accounting are governed by a set of principles and concepts procedures in accounting. All aspects of accounting must be handled with integrity, honesty, and ethical behavior. Not only are there many legal issues involved in managing finances, but there are many personal issues as well. Businesses and individuals base important decisions on the results of the accounting process. The system used in keeping records has therefore evolved to minimize the possibility for errors.

When you own your own business, you need to know how well your business is doing. A business will use financial statements to decide if the company is doing well. Financial statements have to do with the finances of a company and its assets. Learning how to read and understand financial statements takes practice, knowledge, and time.

A balance sheet is a financial statement that shows the assets, liabilities, and owners' equity. Assets are the items or possessions which a business owns. Liabilities are the money that the business owes to someone else. The balance sheet formula for net worth is assets minus liabilities plus net worth or owners' equity.

Accounts are any single item or entry used on a financial statement or used in record keeping in a business. For example, if you charge some paper at Carpenter Paper Co., you will have an account payable titled "Carpenter Paper Co." If you kept track of your advertising expense, you will have an account payable titled "advertising expense."

Net worth is the amount of money a person has to use to start a business. This includes any profits made less any withdrawals. Net worth is also known by other names. It is also called "owners' equity," "owners' capital," or "working capital."

Petty cash is an amount of cash that a company has on hand in the store. It is usually kept in a cash register or cashbox.

Inventory is the amount of material the company has available to sell or use.

Accounts receivable is the money that different customers owe to your business or charge accounts.

Accrued expenses are the expenses that have not been paid such as earnings or wages of employees that have not been yet been paid or payroll taxes that have not yet been paid to the government.

Gross profits are the amount of money the business takes in before expenses are subtracted. The cost of sales, however, have been subtracted.

Cost of sales or cost of goods sold is the amount of money the business has to pay for the materials or goods it sells.

Expenses are the items that the business has to spend money on: rent, utilities, salaries, advertising, travel expenses, and other costs for business operations.

Interest expense is the amount the harness must pay in addition to the money it borrows for the cost of the loan.

Net profit is the money the business has made after all the expenses and costs have been subtracted.

Inventory management is necessary for owners who want to maintain a stocking service for quick turnaround to help ensure total customer satisfaction. The "fill rate" of any item on a managed inventory list must be maintained to avoid shortages of frequently used items. Even when utilizing an inventory management system, occasional shortages will occur.

To be successful in today's fast-paced, highly-competitive environment, shops need to have the necessary parts in stock or have reliable suppliers to meet customer demands at a moment's notice.

However, some shops refuse to have any stocked items at all. Frequently, the philosophy here is that the shop does not want to tie up money in unused inventory. The plus side of this philosophy is that the shop does not spend much time or money on an inventory system since it depends solely on its parts suppliers to stock the items the shop moves frequently.

The benefits of keeping significant quantities of parts in stock are not always clear. The financial benefit must be high enough to justify not only the cash expense but also the time and money spent to manage the inventory.

Some shop owners think simple "garage-keeper" software programs are the best buys for inventory management. Some use customized programs, and others rely on integrated shop management systems or similar "do-all" package systems.

Tire stores tend to use some of the best inventory systems on the market. The reason is not surprising considering the fluid amount of the tire business and the importance of having the right tires in stock. Custom-designed software programs are the most often used programs for these businesses. The biggest plus of having one of these systems, according to several shop owners, is having a comprehensive, proven inventory management system that tracks problems areas and automatically makes corrections when needed.

Comprehensive business software programs that incorporate inventory functions as merely one of many features are not always the best choice for a shop. Companies should take time to search out an appropriate program and establish that the program will perform the functions needed. By asking questions, you're sure to find out which systems have been working well for your fellow association members.

I started the new millennium with a well-devised management plan and made that plan part of my business operation. By counting on a quality inventory management program to bring me into the next century, I will be able to facilitate the success that comes from good overall management techniques.

A promissory note is a promise made in writing to pay a specified sum of money on demand or at a given date to a designated person. In most cases, it is a promise to repay money that has been lent for business purposes. The sum of money that is to be repaid is usually more than the sum lent. The difference is the interest on the loan. The person who signs the note is called the maker. The person

A WINNING BUSINESS

to whom it is made payable is called the payee. The date on which payment is due is the redemption date.

A note containing the words "order of" before the name of the payee is negotiable and may be assigned or passed to a third party who is known as the holder. To complete the assignment, the payee must endorse the note by signing his or her name at the back of the note, and then ideally informing the maker in writing. The holder may in turn transfer the note back to another person by endorsing it. This can go on until the redemption date is reached, at which time the note is deemed to have matured. These transfers take place because promissory notes are bought and sold.

Many promissory notes are backed by collateral, which is some form of property offered as security or a guarantee of repayment of the loan. The collateral is held by the payee and retimed when the note has been paid; if the maker fails to pay, the payee may sell the collateral, talking the costs of the sale and the sum due on the note before handing the balance, if any, to the maker.

Promissory notes are rare today because credit terms are generally offered in commercial contracts for buying and selling goods.

A note is negotiable when it is made payable to "bearer" or includes the word "order*," like the one given above. When a note has been transferred by endorsement, the person in possession of the note is known as the holder. The holder can transfer it to another person by endorsing it, and so on indefinitely, just as a bank check can be transferred. When the note falls due, the holder looks to the maker for payment. The law protects the holder under almost all conditions, including some kinds of fraud or cheating by the payee.

An endorser is liable in case the maker fails to pay the note when it falls due. The endorser is served with a notice called a protest. It is signed by a notary of public, and one copy is sent to each endorser if there is more than one.

Negotiable instruments are a type of legal exchange or document that is either a promise or an order to pay money.

A draft is a written order drawn by one party, directing a second party to pay a definite amount of money to a third party.

The general rule for computing interest is interests = principle x annual rate x period of time the note is.

Different types of companies require different methods of accounting consistent with their particular needs. Plants need to manage more than just rotating and reciprocating machinery; they need a management platform that allows them to integrate not only various condition monitoring techniques but also all the various production assets in their plants: things like valves, boilers, heat exchangers, instrumentation, and any other physical equipment assets used in their processes. The primary elements of such a system include condition monitoring, maintenance management, and reliability management modules with integration to one another and to production and business control systems.

Asset condition management collects measurement data, both actual and derived from the plant's production assets. It will provide diagnostic tools to assess the condition of the assets and identify asset faults. It then makes this information available to other systems where appropriate action can be taken. The condition management system tells you what is wrong with the asset, the severity of the problem, and what to do about it. It also tells you when no problem exists.

Reliability management provides such as diagrams, charts, etc. for statistically analyzing asset reliability and for generating reliability metrics. Reliability management tells you where to focus in the overall asset management initiative and measures success relative to goals.

Maintenance management automates the maintenance process, records maintenance history, and manages maintenance resources. These systems have been known as computerized maintenance management systems. The role of this module is the condition of the system and management and reliability of it. The role of this is to identify where to focus the maintenance resources.

It should be readily obvious that decision-making in a plant draws upon all three systems. A condition management system might identify a problem and recommend a corrective action, but the maintenance management system would have to be consulted as well. Is there a need for spare parts and tool available? If not, what is the lead time for ordering and the cost? Are the right personnel available? How much time should be allocated for the repair, and are there other maintenance activities that should be performed at the same time? The reliability management system can analyze historical maintenance activity data to uncover patterns and recurring root causes that might otherwise go unnoticed. It can also identify where the biggest reliability problems are occurring and which problems should be tackled first for the best cost/benefit ratio.

Payroll provides for check processing, payroll accounting, and quarterly reporting. Payroll can be processed weekly, biweekly, semimonthly, monthly, semiannually, or annually. It allows payroll hours to be distributed to a specific job. Pay is automatically based on the employees' information or by the wage scale a particular job class.

Information for every quarter is stored and can be accessed at any time. Federal and state quarterly reports can be printed to provide you with the information you need for your quarterly tax returns. Information for each year is stored and can be acquired anytime. W-2 forms can be printed for all employees at the end of the year.

401k contributions can be withheld from employee wages and detailed reporting of information on employer contentions is available.

Union deductions, pays, and benefits can be recorded through payroll and reported on various reports, on paychecks, and W-2s.

The general ledger entries are automatically made for each payroll cycle to appropriate general ledger accounts which you have set up throughout the payroll system.

Job costing is automatically made for each payroll cycle to appropriate general ledger accounts which you have set up throughout the payroll system.

Does the availability of long-term financing affect a firm's productivity by facilitating access to more productive technologies and capital accumulation? Or does the less intense monitoring and lesser fear of liquidation associated with long-term debt actually reduce productivity?

Recent theory increasingly emphasizes the association of short-term debt with higher-quality firms and better incentives. The possibility of premature liquidation, for example, may serve as a disciplinary device to better improve the firm's performance. At the same time, the role of long-term debt, especially when it is heavily subsidized, is being rethought because so many development banks are plagued with nonperforming loans and doubts about the selection criteria used in allocating funds.

Long-term debt is very unevenly distributed and almost 30 percent of firms never have access to it during the period studied. Large firms are more likely to have access to long-term debt than small firms. The former are on average more profitable.

Operating profits do not increase the profitability of receiving long-term credit and may actually decrease it. This suggests that the mechanism used to allocate long-term resources may be flawed. The allocation problem was worse for directed credit. There is some evidence that after financial liberation, the problem was less severe.

There is a strong positive association between asset maturity and debt maturity, a matching of assets and liabilities. Shorter-term loans are not conducive to greater productivity, while long-term loans may lead to improvements in productivity. While long-term loans may positively affect the quality of capital accumulation, they do not have an impact on the amount of fixed investments.

A partnership is an association formed by two or more people to carry on business. The people usually agree either in writing or verbally to become partners. But people who run a business together and share the profits are usually considered partners, even if they do not intend to be.

All partners have equal rights and obligations in running the business, unless they have agreed on another arrangement. Any disagreement that arises among them is decided by majority vote. Each partner is an agent for the other partners. Ordinarily, therefore, anything a partner does that seems to be carrying on the business in the usual way is binding on the other partners.

All partners share in the profits of the business, but they do not necessarily share equally. The size of each share is agreed upon when the partnership is set up. It depends on how much money or property each contributes to get the business started and on the kind and amount of work each partner is to do. Every partner is expected to devote time to the business. If one does more work than the others, the partners may agree to pay that person a salary in addition to a share of the profits. Unless a system for sharing the debts of the partnership is set up formally, partners share their debts equally.

All the partners must be faithful to one another in their business dealings. No partner may enter into a transaction in the same line of business as the partnership without sharing the profits with other partners. Neither may any partner use funds or property of the partnership as his or her own.

All partners are liable for any debts acquired by the business dealings. These debts are normally paid out of funds or property belonging to the business. If they cannot be paid in this way, any other property of a partner can be taken by the people to whom the debt is owed. A person can lose money by belonging to a partnership that fails. To avoid such a loss, many states allow limited partnerships. A limited partner may not take an active part in running the business but is liable only for the amount of money he or she has invested. If a person wants to take part in running a business and still not risk losing more than he or she has invested, that person must form a corporation.

A corporation is a person or group who obtained a charter, giving them certain legal rights and privileges. A corporation can own property, buy and sell, manufacture, and bring lawsuits as if its members were one person. Business corporations are the most common types of corporations. Other types are municipal, government-owned, quasi-public, nonprofit, and single person corporations.

Business corporations make up about 15 percent of all business enterprise in the United States. Partnerships and individual proprietorships form the remainder. However, business corporations account for more than 75 percent of all business assets. Business corporations may be public or private.

The most common type is the public corporation, which obtains funds by selling ownership shares called capital stock to a large number of people.

There are two varieties of stock, preferred and common. Preferred stock does not extend voting rights in the corporation but gives holders first claim on the company assets after debts are paid. Common stock gives stockholders voting rights. Corporations reward stockholders for then giving them part of the profits. These payments are called dividends.

The two major kinds of income taxes are individual income taxes and corporate income taxes. Individual income taxes, also called personal income tax, are levied on the income of the individual. Corporate income taxes are applied to the earnings of corporations.

An income tax may be progressive, where the more money a person earns, the higher the percentage of tax will be or proportional, where you pay the same levels of tax for all levels of income.

Investments that involve the exchange in currency from one country to another or the debts between two countries will use foreign exchange rates and instruments, such as bank drafts, checks, and telegraph orders, which are the principal means of international transactions.

The rate of exchange is the price in local currency of one unit of foreign currency and is determined by the relative supply and demand of the currency in the foreign exchange market.

The cash flow projection is one of the most useful financial statements because it looks forward. Both the income statement and the balance sheet illustrate what has happened in the past. While the past is important, it is more important that you have an idea what the future holds and that you plan accordingly.

Business owners should assemble a cash flow plan to budget their cash resources and to make sure the business owner's expectations are realistic. Preferably, a banker or CPA will review the projection to make sure that it is an accurate tool for your business.

The cash flow statement is a very important tool for the investors of the company and for the creditors. The impact of current cash flow statements have an impact on the amount of debt banks will allow a company to have and the amount of a new capital that investors will extend. Realistic, honest, and fair evaluations of the future of the company will best ensure the proper management and funding for projects and payments for current debts.

Financial accounting involves the preparation of a business's financial statements mainly for users outside the business. These reports are used by owners and potential owners of a business and by people who have loaned a company money. Some government agencies that regulate business and the stock market require companies to submit financial statements to them.

Management accounting and the services that provide the information consist of a variety of activities that many accountants perform. These activities and services include the design and installation of computerized financial information systems, assistance in setting up employee pension plans, and the planning of an individual's personal finances.

Accounting systems are created for the purpose of providing sophisticated, high-quality, client-oriented, software that CPAs and accounting professionals can use to develop easily understood reports that assess the individual or corporation's history of accounts.

These accounting systems help managers in developing the past histories of assets and liabilities, loans, and payment histories and assess the future direction of personal or corporate procedures.

A formal in-process costing system provides for guidance of activities and for attaining the objectives of producing a maximum of goods and services at the least amount of cost. The formal in-process cost accounting method is designed to accumulate those costs that are under the control of local management. Typically, the system manager controls all costs that are funded by appropriations for funds provided to the accounting entity.

In-process costing systems provides a tool for determining, reporting, analyzing, and controlling the cost of a particular process or series of procedures. It classifies, records, presents, and interprets in a significant manner the material, labor, and overhead expenses necessary to produce a product or service.

Job costing deals with the calculation of invoicing available based on price sheets and labor rates for individual job. Many systems are available that establish an unlimited number of transactions for each job. Distribution breakdown by job phase and job division are also made possible. By understanding these details, future predictions of other jobs can be defined and more readily accessible.

Cost-volume-profit analysis is a predictive tool used by managers to plan and control the activities of a business. With this tool, the management can forecast future costs, revenues, and profits at various levels of business activity.

Some questions answered by cost-volume-profit analysis include the following. What level of sales most be reached in order to break even? What will happen to net income if unit selling prices are reduced by a dollar and unit volume increases by 10 percent, etc.? These type of questions can be answered by understanding relationships among revenues, costs, and estimated unit sales volume.

The first step in cost-volume-profit analysis is to know how cost behave in response to changes in some activity. By plotting both costs and revenues at various levels of volume on the same graph, a cost-volume-profit graph may be developed which illustrates the expected profit or loss at any level of volume.

In my particular business in the building business, I was able to find a particular program that enabled me to easily keep proper records of income, expenses, tax records, bank finance, inventory, and profit and loss statements. I could easily print and document the necessary information that made the company a success through the years.

As computers and programs improved, I also developed new methods of properly running my corporation. Through the years, I learned techniques that enabled me to keep the company running efficient and productive.

Modern Man, Artist, and Architecture

The modern man exists in the twenty-first century. But what comprises this complex human form? As a science, the evolution of the human species is as follows: the human or first species of primate; the *Homo habilis* first skilled man; *Homo erectus* or first primate to walk on two legs; *Homo sapiens* from Africa or wise man; and the Paleolithic period's Neanderthal man.

The advances made during the New Stone Age were as follows: human farming, animal husbandry. These dramatically changed the way of living during the Neolithic age and continued until the modern era and modern man.

Neolithic society for women consisted mostly of household chores: spinning, weaving, pottery, and sewing of clothes for the family or clan. Bearing children remains to this day the most important factor in society from the Neolithic society to today's modern man.

The size of one's family during the mentioned periods was a sign of wealth and strength. Even today, society having a family of size is an indication of wealth.

The first civilizations arose in five different areas of the globe: Mesopotamia, Egypt, India, China, and Mesoamerica. The city-state that took shape in these areas of the globe had complex populations, complex social organizations, and had advanced technical skills. During this period, iron replaced bronze for tools and farming implements around the globe.

Today's modern man faces many new challenges in the twenty-first century. In the year 2019, mankind is on the cusp, the dawning of yet another new age. The age of the electric car. The science community all supports this change from an oil-driven economy to an economy based on electricity, and most likely nuclear power.

In the year 2019, America in particularly have advance wind turbine power to supply about 5.5 percent of the total electric output. Solar provides 1.66 percent of the total output of power.

Nuclear power from ninety-eight reactors provides 65 percent of the total electric output in America. Natural gas and coal comprise the rest of the total electric power. The United States of America has *not* built the twenty-first century reactor yet.

The fast integral reactor was designed in America, but three phases of testing were never completed. Meanwhile, China in particular has built thirty-eight in China from our design and is building twelve more today.

Throughout Europe and other parts of the globe, more have been built by China than any other nation.

In the twenty-first century, America has to lead the way with our nuclear security team of IAEA to balance and share the most affordable source of electricity in the globe today. This is the most important factor for cleaning up the globe—America's control of the nuclear power plant and its fissile fuel and their production levels around the world.

Fissile fuel is the cheapest material form to create energy on the globe.

Can fissile fuel be made into a nuclear bomb? No. Fissile fuel has been depleted to the point of no return from plutonium and thus *cannot* be made back into a nuclear bomb.

Rogue states' arid terrorists could produce a dirty bomb with this low-yield radioactive material. However, the same thing is today possible by rogue states and terrorists. The net sum is a zero net gain.

Robert Frost was a unique individual who witnessed firsthand the miracle of life that he found all around him. He was a dairy fanner at the turn of the century and wrote many famous poems. Two of which will be discussed in this essay. Those we will try to understand will be "For Once, Then, Something" and "Design." These two poems have symbolisms that lead the reader to a deeper understanding of the world we live and the world to come.

The symbols he describes found in nature are metaphors to describe the conflict within life itself and the skeptical side of what our minds can possibly understand.

"For Once, Then, Something" speaks of the relationship of what Frost sees in life and what is blurred from his reality in life. He begins with the acknowledgment that others taunt him for his search for the meaning of life, which is represented by him having knelt at a well to see the reflection and never being to see past it.

"Others taunt me with having knelt at well-curbs." This first line can be described as soul-searching in many places for the well of life or God. And while there are many religions, the search for God continues. The mocking others see in this must have frustrated him, and yet the fact he was willing to kneel before God represented by the well gives the reader the first part of the search for inner peace and the sanctity we all search for.

"Always wrong to the light, so never seeing," represents a search we as humans can never fully understand, but take faith in the feet. God is ever-present even in the smallest of the many wonders He has given us as a human race to try to comprehend—though the light He speaks of is found in death and the beyond. We are always wrong to the light because we have never been resurrected; only one can say, "I am the light."

"Deeper down in the well than where the water. / Gives me back in a shining surface picture," represents outbirth into this world, and the voyage he now, at this moment in time, finds himself—perhaps halfway through his own existence in this world. He sees only a reflection of himself, and perhaps the deeds forever recorded in time. For it is said, "Our reflection is that of God, but in such an imperfect form, we all are condemned to die but once." Frost has a deeper understanding of his place in time and the understanding of the life and death cycle. The picture he sees in the reflection must be that of his deeds on earth, and many that only he and God understands.

"Me myself in the summer heaven godlike. / Looking out of a wreath of fern and cloud puffs." Frost, looking deep into his soul and deep into the well, finds himself to be godlike in the reflections he sees with the puffs of clouds overhead, yet looking down into his future, he is not immortal. A deeper realization begins to take place as we read further into the poem, perhaps of the time gone by and the realization of what lies ahead. He is searching for answers, and that must be the beginning. For he sees all God has created and all God has condemned.

"Once, when trying with chin against a well-curb, I discerned, as I thought, beyond the picture…" This must have been a very troubling time for Frost. Obviously depressed enough to lay his head down on the well, he was trying to understand himself and his reflection, perhaps his own lack of understanding of life and his existence. Is a picture worth a thousand words? Particularly when you are discerning your own existence in this life in which we are given choices and paths and guidance from our own spiritual being: our mind, our soul.

"Through the picture, a something white, uncertain, / Something more of the depths—and then I lost it." Frost could almost reach out and see beyond tomorrow to the future to truly understand the place in time God created for him. Then, like most, the fleeting moment is gone. So much like life itself, I guess. Perhaps this something "white" was the spirit that binds all mankind but beyond the depths of human understanding and out of reach of Frost himself. But perhaps the search is greater than never trying and continuing like sheep without a shepherd.

"Water came to rebuke the too clear water. / One drop fell from a fern, and lo, a ripple. / Shook whatever it was lay there at the bottom…" The answers Frost searched for were within his grasp, and yet it was the water that fell and shattered the image of what lay beyond. Water was a symbol of life, forgiveness, and yet it was never God's intent to let mankind fully understand His reasons for our place in the history, past and future; for God redeems, and God punishes—something we as mere mortals should never know.

A WINNING BUSINESS

In the last two lines, Frost simply says, "Blurred it, blotted it out. What was that whiteness? / Truth? A pebble of quartz? For once, then, something." Frost never grasp what he searched for, or if he did, he never understood. For who can truly understand God, the whiteness, except in death and the afterlife.

Ralph Waldo Emerson also had searched for the comparison of nature and its spiritual facts. He was "an American essayist and poet, born in Boston. Seven of his ancestors were ministers, and his father was the minister of the First Church (Unitarian) of Boston." His most detailed statement of belief was reserved for his first published book, *Nature*.

The poem "Design," by Robert Frost—the reader finds expressions of nature and the symbolism of the human spirit in the design of life, its destruction, and how life is passed on and begins again.

The poem begins, "I found a dimpled spider, fat and white, / On a white heal-all, holding up a moth / Like a white piece of rigid satin cloth…" Robert Frost is describing what he found and using it to symbolize much more than just a moth caught in a spider's web.

The spider, which symbolizes all that have gone before us, being fat and white, has built its web upon a plant that has blossoms reputed to have healing powers. The spider symbolized God and perhaps heaven, a place where we are called too and caught up from inception. With no irony, the web is placed on a plant with healing powers, powers of redemption. The web is as rigid as satin cloth, showing us the certainty of death.

"Assorted characters of death and blight / Mixed ready to begin the morning right, / Like the ingredients of a witches' broth— / A snow-drop spider, a flower like a froth, / And dead wings carried like a paper kite."

In the second stanza, you find all the people or characters that have been caught in the trap of death. This appetite nature has for people and all creation seems to Frost as being caught in a web, mixed cultures being judged repeatedly, daily. Again, the spider has his web built on a flower with healing powers, and the wings he speaks of might be the reincarnation into angels that he can see within this web of the life cycle. The just in God's eyes might be carried to heaven like "a paper kite."

"What had that flower to do with being white, / The wayside blue and innocent heal-all? / What brought the kindred spider to that height, / Then steered the white moth thither in the night? / What but design of darkness to appall?— / If design govern in a thing so small."

The last stanza raises Frost's questions as to the nature of the flower being white. A symbol of what many say they see at death—a white light calling them to this redemption found in death some would say heaven. The spider has built his web at a great height and has called all in the night. This symbolism of light found in heaven and of darkness found in death and the calling at the will of God to a thing so small as a moth or a life of a person reminds us of the temporal amount of time we have and that the whole world is but a small part of God's creation.

"Robert Frost's importance as a poet derives from the power and memorability of particular poems… He combines lyric and dramatic poetry in blank verse." His reputation as a major poet is secure, and from his beginnings on a farm to his renowned literary works, he unquestionably succeeded in realizing his life's ambition: to write "a few poems it will be hard to get rid of."

Both Robert Frost and Ralph Waldo Emerson were a part of the transcendental movement in American literature. Both had intense study in philosophy, religion, and literature. They exemplified the facts of nature and spiritual facts that bring the world into a different kind of light. The conflict of life as a struggle and the tools of master poets Frost and Emerson both delighted the people of their time, and of future generations a poem of Robert Frost's, "The Gift Outright" was even "read at the inauguration of John F. Kennedy."

In *The Education of Henry Adams*, he describes being born into a very distinguished family in Massachusetts not far from the capitol building. Being from a family of a minister of Unitarianism, he is both handicapped and finds advantage in his birthright. This internal struggle for his independence and the way the world would judge

A WINNING BUSINESS

him is the foundation for *The Education of Henry Adams*. This is a book about the world of the eighteen hundreds: the lifestyle, conditions, and political policies that shaped him and forced the realization of who he is.

Henry Adams's great-grandfather was John Adams, and his grandfather was John Quincy Adams. Both were United States Presidents. His father, Charles Francis Adams, was a congressman, diplomat, and a public servant with great talent and merit. He was born in 1838, a time when the Albany Railroad connected Boston with New York, and Cunard Steamers began regular transatlantic steamship service between Boston and Europe.

By the age of six, he developed scarlet fever; he nearly died. This near-death experience shaped his education, and certain values were established that later in life would prove useful. Sickness in childhood had no boundaries, for rich or poor alike were at the mercy of a God, a God that had his reasons for everything within the world Henry Adams knew. He sought a greater importance of true knowledge, and from this, a point of view of education grew throughout his life. From this, he questioned the judgment of the world he lived and began to shape the world to come.

As a boy, he understood that "politics, as a practice, whatever its professions, had always been the systematic organization of hatreds, and Massachusetts politics had been as harsh as the climate." This climate was prevalent and cultivated in his education as a young child. Could a country such as America claim "freedom" when even as a youth he can see the injustice of the society in which he lived?

This was the question that was ever present in the mind of Henry Adams. The two seasons he saw represent the ruling class and the underclass that he was much aware of. This was the beginning of the education of Henry Adams and the theme that runs throughout this book. He looked beyond the world he lived and saw the lack of free choice many Americans dealt with in their day-to-day life. "Boys are wild animals, rich in the treasures of sense, but the New England boy had a wider range of motions than boys of more equitable climates." For Henry the idea of servants was blasphemy, even though he was a part of society in which this injustice prevailed. This injustice was a curse and brought chaos to his life. Henry Adams could sit alongside a president, his grandfather, and remember how his great-grandfather "pledged his life, his fortune, and his sacred honor," to secure the independence of this country. What would the future bring to this land where so many had given so much?

In 1854, young Adams, for the purpose of future advancement, was to attend Harvard College. This was the "next regular step" in the life chosen by his society to become a respectable citizen and a useful leader. The school may have molded a type of character but did not change his will in perceiving leadership and justice. For the school was intolerant of ideologies not found in that time but praised and even flattered the passion in their education of the student. Harvard was, in that day, a school of the elite, and naturally this theme was present in their graduates. "The Class of 1858, to which Henry Adams belonged, was a typical collection of young New Englanders, quietly penetrating and aggressively commonplace; free from meanness, jealousies, intrigues, enthusiasms, and passions…but little disposed to trust anyone else." This vanity became their law of nature, not to be questioned, judged, or appealed.

Colonel Robert E. Lee, of the Second United States Cavalry, was a Virginian of the eighteenth century as much as Henry Adams was a Bostonian of the same age. Lee was a tall, largely built, handsome, and genial man with a Virginian openness toward the values he had. He commanded and took leadership as habit, and the people understood and did not contest that leadership. This type of belief was held by many in congress, and Henry Adams liked the Virginians. However, there was a distinct difference between the North and South; one might even call it jealousy between the two eighteenth century types of cultures and their beliefs.

The result of the different cultures between the North and South led to the American Civil War. The social instincts and intellectual training of the North and the temperament of the South led to ten years of killing each other. In the end, Henry Adams felt this destruction left both sides betrayed by the diplomats who lost their sons in battle. This savage, ill temper was an excessive waste of energy, but the United States was once again whole, but for a great price. Robert

A WINNING BUSINESS

E. Lee was a gentleman who Henry Adams liked, so he felt the loss and destruction of the South despite his upbringing.

Henry Adams began to have his works printed. First, the college magazines printed his works, and the college societies listened. He was chosen Class Orator, and this was a political as well as a literary success. "Year by year, his position seemed to improve, or perhaps his rivals disappeared..." Henry Adams became a fairly well-trained politician. The people saw in him a representative—the kind they wanted. "The young man—always in search of education—asked himself whether, setting rhetoric aside, this absence of enthusiasm was a defect or a merit..." He was ready to stand toe-to-toe before any audience, whether in America or Europe.

The South was now reconstructed, and urbanization and industrialization came as a result of the Civil War. The coming of capitalism, moneylenders, and railways led to many other developments.

Henry Adams wanted knowledge. This knowledge came from experience, some from formal training and much was a thirst for things to come. His chief interest was developing new motors to make airships feasible. He sought the knowledge of the internal combustion engine, steam generators, and electric current development that brought energy to a rapidly changing America. The discovery of radium advanced science to harness a new power. "The force was wholly new." Henry Adams states, "Here opened another totally new education, which promised to be by far the most hazardous of all."

"When a radioactive chemical is released from a large area, such as an industrial plant, it enters the environment." Perhaps Henry Adams had foresight into the effect industrialization would have on people in the near future. For with the age of industrialization came new threats to life itself, and this perplexing problem would influence human progress and human life.

The atomic bomb would later be developed. "This process of fission released enormous energy in the form of extreme heat and a massive shock wave." This nearly unimaginable destructive force destroys all living matter and contaminates the earth and water. "The secret of education still hid itself somewhere behind ignorance, and one fumbled over it as feebly as ever." Henry Adams saw the effects industrialization had on society after the Civil War and perhaps could see what this new age of science would bring.

> "Man always made, and still makes, grotesque blunders in selecting and measuring forces, taken at random from the heap, but he never made a mistake in the value he set for the whole, which he symbolized as unity and worshipped as God. To this day, his attitude towards it had never changed, though science can no longer give to force a name."
> —Henry Adams.

Architecture contains the truest function of art. This art brings order to the chaotic material of the human experience. The history of these examples can be traced back from the ancient world to modern buildings that serve a function to the human experience.

This definition is applicable enough when we test it on the Parthenon in Athens. The Temple of Athena Parthenos, the Parthenon, was built to house a huge gold and ivory statue of the goddess Athena, patron of the city-state of Athens. This work of art so perfect in order that even in ruins it is the affirmation that all confusion is vanquished within its creation.

Around the middle of the twelfth century, churches began to rise, thrusting new and wonderful forms into the light, growing in height and splendor, and more elaborate in competition with one another. Gothic architecture in Europe from 1200 to 1500 with pointed arches, ribbed vaulting, and flying buttresses transformed Cathedrals into monumental works of art. They summarized spiritual aspirations of the age with the mystical faith symbolized by the soaring forms. This art was achieved with new feats of practical engineering. The great height of the cathedrals, with their hovering apparently weightless stone vaults, demanded building methods more daring than the world had ever known.

The Cathedral of Notre Dame in the heart of Paris, France, is noted as the "World Ambassador of Gothic Cathedrals," and the concept of Gothic is derived from this structure. "In the largest sense of the phrase, the Gothic church emphasized the totality, rather than the complexity, of a concept of the Heavenly Jerusalem." The west front of the cathedral is a classic of the French Gothic style, with three richly carved portals or doorways. The central portal depicts the biblical story of the Last Judgment. The north and south fronts are decorated with two rose windows with circular stained glass. Another rose window, at the west front of the cathedral, is considered a masterpiece of Gothic engineering for its large glass surface area. This enormous rose window is supported by a seemingly delicate web of carved stone tracery. In this sanctuary, the French Emperor Napoleon Bonaparte and the Empress Josephine were crowned in 1804. This monument to France forever preserved the moment of spiritual aspirations of an age full of human evils to rise above, to bring forth a glorious truth—that mystical faith—that is symbolized in this soaring form.

The Sistine Chapel, the Vatican in Rome, Italy, has its walls are adorned with Sandro Botticelli masterpieces, and the ceiling vault displays Michelangelo's thunderous "Last Judgment," with the martyrs, saints, and the blessed on their way to Paradise, which intensifies our experience of desperation and terror. "The tremendous form of the chapel, built by Giovannino dei Dolci for Pope Sixtus IV in 1473 to 1484" is the focus for the many inspirations within.

The Cathedral of St. Peter in France, with its geometric patterns, patterns that are continued on the exterior by the geometrical forms of the buttresses supporting them. "This Euclidean geometry held an honored position in the Middle Ages as an art form, in on of itself." This art solved problems of covering the spaces of unprecedented height and width and allowed the observer to parallel the philosophical existence of a mystical God in the nonmystical terms of the cathedral.

Today, the Empire State Building, with its steel frame and stone cladding, with low-key Art Deco and effective use of setbacks to emphasize its 102 towering floors, transforms architecture into a titanic sculpture that lights up at night like scattered jewels. It stands in lonely dignity in the midriff of Manhattan, a sentinel by land, a reassuring landmark by air. "The Empire State Building, like most art deco skyscrapers, was modernistic, not modernist. It was deliberately less pure, more flamboyant and populist than European theory allowed. It appeared to be a sculpted or a modeled mass, giving to the business imagery a substantial character."

"Manhattan's only remaining great gateway, Grand Central Terminal, was built to house Cornelius Vanderbilt's railroad network and stands as a functional art structure." Reed and Stem were commissioned for its functional aspects of design, while the Vanderbilts added Whitney Warren, trained in the Beaux Arts, to be responsible for the aesthetics of the station. Grand Central Terminal was modeled after the Roman imperial baths, and because of its size, invites comparison to the Paris Opera House. Outside, the limestone-clad facade with its Roman triumphant arch that symbolizes the triumph of the railroad and the nation's premier urban development, whose high standards of design and interconnections preceded Rockefeller Center by two decades. With its great arched windows and barrel-vaulted concourse containing a celestial ceiling mural to its extravagant marble floors, Grand Central is getting better with age. With the help of Jacquelyn Kennedy Onassis and her public statements to save and preserve Grand Central, a restoration project of enormous scale has brought greater function to this tremendous form of art. New retail, restaurant, and office facilities have been added along with the restoration. Grand Central is the truest function of art and contains one of the nation's greatest public sculptures: Jules-Alexis Coutane's heroic statue of Mercury in front of an eagle, flanked by Minerva and Hercules that perch atop the terminal peering south down Park Avenue.

But what of the art found on a canvas? Art that shimmers with color and glows with budding fertility. The image is there for us to glance at, elaborate on, and its appeal is immediate. From a blank canvas forms ranging from a dramatic portrait to a landscape, to the abstract, the displays of beauty, personality, and emotion are forever captured in a single moment in time.

Rembrandt Van Rijn never visited Italy, but by the time, he settled in Amsterdam in 1631, he was developing the latest in Baroque painting. While his early work displayed thunderous use of light and shade with dramatic figures filling the pictures surface, "Rembrandt's later works would search out more reflective moods and he discovered a new and glorious freedom in brushstroke." Of all the Baroque masters, Rembrandt worked in complex layers. He developed a technique of "building up a picture from the back to the front with delicate glazes that allowed light actually to permeate his backgrounds and reflect off the white underpainting and generously applied body colors which mimicked the effect of solid bodies in space."

Pierre Auguste Renoir, an early twentieth century French impressionist painter most noted for the female nude that were intimate and radiant. "He was recognized by his own critics as one of the greatest impressionist painters of his tune." Renoir brought harmony with his lines, brilliance of color, and intimate charm. His wide variety of subjects, from portraits to family groups and landscapes, all exemplify this. As a child, he designed paintings in a porcelain factory. Later his works were influenced by Claude Monet's use of light and the romantic painter Eugene Delacroix and his use of color. Renoir's most famous work *Madame Georges Charpentier and Her children*, where he used his mastery of figure painting and light, depicts the lustrous, pearly color of the skin and is a true representation of feminine grace.

Perhaps no other late twentieth-century artist has been as loved by so many as Norman Rockwell—the grand old man of American art that embraced the simple aspects of American life, whose art is embraced by many who may not think of themselves as art lovers. While his critics said his art was trivial and he observed the obvious while avoiding darker subjects, they cannot deny Rockwell was a painter for the everyday American. His images depicts everyday dreams, hopes, and patriotic images that captured the American Dream.

Pablo Picasso stands as the indisputable genius of twentieth-century art, whose commodities brought to him fame and wealth. "His paintings, etchings, pottery, sketches, indeed, anything he scribbled upon brought small fortunes even as he produced them." Picasso transcended the need for money because "whatever he wished to own, he could acquire by drawing it." Picasso harnessed the developing mass media in an unprecedented experiment in self-promotion. His sentimental works in the Blue and Rose Periods and later with distorted "Cubism," he used constantly varying aspects of reality to define an array of subjects.

These are all great works of art—only a few, in the many thousands of artists and artworks, found all around the world. But can we really say they contain the truest function of art? They are all beautiful to behold, have a range of interest, and display a variety of techniques, but what function do they hold in any society? They can be owned by private collectors or placed in museums, but to what extent do they shape the human existence or serve a purpose to those who enjoy their form? In all reality and fairness to the art and the artist, they do not serve as the greatest function of art, for that is found only in the tangible, earthly forms we call architecture. For architecture is the medium in which all art resides and its form is art itself.

Science and Global Warming

If only half of the carbon dioxide emitted into the atmosphere is recycled by Earth, what happens to the other half? Does the other half pose a problem or is the controversy about global warming just a lot of hot air? In the case study *Life in the Greenhouse, the Effects of Global Warming*, the authors Newton and Dillingham take us on a journey of scientific facts, scientific speculations, possible consequences, controversies, and ethical values, all related to the broad concept we call global warming or the greenhouse effect.

A greenhouse is kept warm because energy coming in from the sun in the form of visible sunlight is able to pass through the glass and heats the soil and plants inside. But energy that is emitted from the soil and plants in the form of invisible infrared radiation is not able to easily pass through the glass of the greenhouse. Some of the infrared heat energy is trapped inside. This is the main reason why a greenhouse is warmer inside than outside. The atmosphere surrounding the Earth is made up of many different gasses. Some of these gasses such as carbon dioxide, methane nitrous oxide, and ozone act like a glass of a greenhouse. They let solar energy from the sun pass through but prevent the exit of reflected radiation, thus, warming the Earth. This natural cycle is what keeps everything alive, and without it, we would die.

The level of the atmospheric gasses have remained relatively constant throughout the Earth's history; however, scientists have speculated for decades that the amount of gasses released by man is causing higher concentrations of the atmospheric gasses which traps additional heat, creating the greenhouse effect, also called global warming. This alleged greenhouse effect became a controversy when Dr. Jim Hansen, a highly respected scientist of NASA, testified before Congress in June 1988 that sufficient evidence pointed to a greenhouse effect. Many scientists disagreed on the greenhouse effect, and those who disagreed thought that Dr. Hansen's testimony lacked evidence. The Intergovernmental Panel in Climate Control (IPCC) partially backed up Dr. Hansen's statement seven years later when it stated in a report that global warming is in effect caused partially by human activity. Today, Dr. Hansen's testimony is credited as the single most important event that raised awareness that human activities can cause changes in the climate. As more scientific research was presented as evidence of global warming, the apocalyptic theories and computer prediction models followed. Melted ice caps causing higher sea levels, droughts in wet regions, and floods in dry regions would force hundreds of millions of people to relocate, spelling natural and economic disasters worldwide.

The opposition, those who disagree with the global warming theories and the cause of it, have presented their own scientific evidence stating that the methods used to measure the global warming are incorrect. Others consider the evidence of global warming is insufficient and speculative and that more substantial evidence is required. Some speculate that our planet is in a natural cycle and that estimated temperature increases of 1–3 degrees every century may not he caused by human activity.

Global warming or not, we are faced with substantial changes in nature as animals have become extinct or changed behavior and habitat due climate changes. In the north and south Arctic regions, more ice melts every summer, and less ice freezes during wintertime. These drastic natural changes are evidently caused by atmospheric changes; however, the cause or source of the atmospheric changes remains controversial.

Supporters of the global warming theory believe that increased concentrations of greenhouse gasses are the cause of the global warming and the major source of these gasses is human activity. Some scientists claim that carbon dioxide is the greatest contributor to global warming, and that human activity is accountable for releasing twice as much carbon dioxide into the atmosphere than the Earth in the form of oceans, forests, and plants can absorb thus causing the increased concentrations. Studies have shown that in order to decrease greenhouse gasses, human activities must emit less carbon dioxide and other greenhouse gasses in order to slow down or stop the global warming process. This brings us to perhaps the core of the problem! Energy use.

Energy production is the spinal cord of our world economy; thus, the energy usage and availability is very important to every country. Some countries are less willing to work toward reductions in emissions, which promoted the creation of the United Nations Conferences on Global Climate Change first held in 1992. The conferences consist of UN members, which all have pledged to reduce carbon dioxide emissions in accordance with the amounts agreed at each conference. The most successful, a time case study publication, was the Kyoto conference in 1997, which called for the greatest reduction in emissions since the conferences.

The opinions on the global warming theory and its cause are diversified among our group members. We have all interpreted the chapter in accordance to our ethical values and logic. We are a group of supporters and opponents of the theory based on different reasoning. In view of this diversity, we have decided to enclose a quotation from each member, reflecting the members' views on the above issues.

"Manufacturing processes used in industry and agriculture and the burning of fossil fuels have increased the amount of these gasses being released into the atmosphere. Over the last two hundred years, there has been a 40 percent increase in carbon dioxide concentrations. This enhanced greenhouse effect means that the planet is gradually getting warmer and warmer."

"How do we control global warming? The good news is that the solutions are clear. Most of our electricity comes from decades' old, dirty coal-burning power. These dinosaurs can be phased out and replaced with cleaner burning plants. Relying more on renewable energy sources, such as wind, solar power, and hydrogen fuel cells, would drastically reduce global warming pollution. We have a responsibility, as individuals and as a nation, to lead the world toward slashing emissions of carbon dioxide and other heat-trapping gasses. We have the solutions to this problem—but we have to begin using them now."

"It is hard to prove that some of the things going on, like extinction, are due to the global warming effect. However, it is hard to argue that nothing is really happening when we have terrible natural events, such as severe flooding or droughts. It is hard to brush off global warming as an effect that is happening simply due to time, because look at what is happening in our environment."

"When we are only spending 1 percent of the budget on energy conservation, I think we may be in trouble at some point. Although our energy sources and environment may not seem like a critical issue, it really is. The difference is that it will slowly show the damage over the years, so people are not as aware. At some point in time, it is going to be a very serious situation that is very visible to the eye. We need to take the time and money now to make necessary changes to save our environment."

"Studies of temperature records dating back more than a century have seemed to indicate a rise in global temperature of around 0.5 °C, with much of it occurring since the late 1970s. This has led many scientists to believe that global warming is under way, with the finger of blame usually pointed at man-made pollution such as carbon dioxide. 'While it is evident that the temperatures are rising, we do not have the data necessary to know if this is caused by what we are doing now or if this is just a cyclical cycle of the Earth.'"

"There seems to be a lot of speculation about the causes and effects of global warming but not much concrete evidence in support of or against it. I can see why it is difficult for governments to decide how to act on the subject when nobody really knows for certain what the outcome really will be. However, I do agree with the author that even though we cannot be positive on the outcome, we can at least work together to try and come up with some solutions."

A WINNING BUSINESS

"It is obvious to me that there is still a lot of research that needs to be done on the topic. Every country on Earth needs to work at reducing emissions as this is a global issue, not just one for a few nations. Our nations need to continue to meet together and develop ideas to reduce carbon dioxide emissions. The government should make some kind of incentive to manufacturers and buyers of products that reduce the wear and tear on the environment. The government should also work to educate the people as to the issues being laced and the reasons for wanting to work towards reducing emissions."

"The scientific facts are pointing towards increased global warming due in part to the massive amount of carbon dioxide we humans release into the atmosphere. We produce twice the amount of carbon dioxide than Earth can absorb; we have a balancing problem, and minds and attitudes must change in order to prevent further climate problems in the future. Changing minds however is difficult, especially in our industrialized energy addictive world, where we are pulled out of our comfort zone as soon as a brown-out hits us. We must work from both ends by reducing emissions while creating biological sinks that can absorb more carbon dioxide. Carbon dioxide is in every living matter as an element, and I would like to see a technology that can absorb/store carbon dioxide and turn in back into a solid element. I think we have the ability to develop technology to clean up the mess we have created. We just need to unlock the desire on governmental and international levels."

Global warming is one of our toughest environmental challenges, threatening the health of our people, wildlife, and economies around the world. We have the know-how to start fixing the problem, but we have to start soon. Decisions we make today will affect the planet for years to come.

The problem is carbon dioxide and other heat-trapping pollution that comes mainly from cars, power plants, and other industrial sources that burn gasoline, coal, and other fossil fuels collecting a blanket in the atmosphere. As a result, the planet is getting warmer. Infect, 2002 was the second warmest year on record, according to NASA.

Although Earth's temperatures fluctuate naturally, warming over the past fifty years is the fastest in history. Experts think the trend is accenting. Scientists say that unless global warming emissions are reduced, average US temperatures could be 5 to 10 degrees higher by the end of the century.

Global warming means more air pollution and problems with water supplies as precipitation patterns change, as well as huge threats to ecosystems from the Everglades to the glaciers. There will be hotter, longer heat waves and more intense storm systems. Forests, farms, and cities will face troublesome new pests and more mosquito-borne disease. Scientists say many of these symptoms are already appearing.

Part of the debate over global warming centers on the disparities between the surface temperatures and upper-air temperatures. While the Earth's surface temperature has risen since data has been collected, little, if any warming of the low to mid troposphere, has occurred. The report by the Research Council said despite these differences "the warming trend in the global mean surface temperature observation daring the past twenty years is undoubtedly real and substantially greater than the average tale of warming the twentieth century." (4)

Based on assumptions that concentrations of greenhouse gasses will accelerate and conservative assumptions about how the climate will react to that, computer models suggest that average global surface temperatures will rise between 4.5 and 10.4 degrees by the end of the century. Projecting how the world's climate will change in the future requires estimating the amount of greenhouse gasses produced by burning fossil fuels and other human activities. These gasses often remain trapped in the atmosphere for many years, trapping radiation that would otherwise escape into the atmosphere. The report difficult to predict future changes.

The Intergovernmental Panel on Climate Change (IPCC) concluded that global warming in the last fifty years is likely the result of increases in greenhouse gasses, which accurately reflects the current thinking of the scientific community. However, it also cautioned that uncertainties about this conclusion remain because of the level of natural variability inherent in the climate on time scales from decades to centuries. The report urges the establishment of a vigorous program of basic research to reduce these uncertainties in future climate projections.

The Earth's surface temperature has risen by about 1 degree Fahrenheit in the past century. The surface temperatures have risen at a substantially greater rate than average in the past two decades. These changes observed over the last several decades are likely because of human activities for the most part. It is not known exactly how much of the temperature rise to date is due to human activities, the report says. Climate models do not adequately represent all the processes that contribute to variability of the climate system. A research council report improving the effectiveness of climate modeling identifies the lack of a coherent national climate modeling program and sufficient computing resources and suggests areas for improvement.

Almost all the major greenhouse gases, with the exception of chlorofluorocarbons (CFCs), have both natural and human-induced sources. For example, carbon dioxide is not only formed by decay in plant matter but also by the burning of coal, oil, natural gas, and wood. Methane can be formed by coal mining, using landfills and handling natural gas. Both carbon dioxide and methane are more abundant in the Earth's atmosphere now than at any time in the past 400,000 years. Carbon dioxide is probably the single most important agent contributing to climate changes today. In addition, the other greenhouse gasses combined contribute to climate changes approximately equal to that of carbon dioxide.

The report by the Environmental Protection Agency (EPA) notes a cooling trend in the Earth's stratosphere, documented by satellite data since 1979, is so pronounced that it would be difficult to explain through natural variability alone. The cooling is believed to be partially a result of the buildup of greenhouse gases and the depletion of stratospheric ozone by chlorofluorocarbons, which warms the atmosphere at low levels but cools at its high levels. The use of chlorofluorocarbons (CFC's) was banned in 1996 by the Montreal Protocol.

Climate change and its consequences are likely to have strong regional effects. Some models predict increased tendency for drought in some regions and higher rainfall in others. Crop distributions and forestry will see changes in future years. Water shortages and water quality problems will get worse. These changes will affect human health, as a warmer climate change will lead to mere mosquitoes, ticks, rodents, and other agents that carry diseases as well as asthma antilung disease.

Today, most mainstream scientists and scientific bodies agree that heat-trapping gases like carbon dioxide (C02) have caused temperatures to rise around the globe. Because emissions of heat-trapping gases are expected to increase, scientists predict temperatures to rise dramatically over the next century, resulting in serious harm to life on our planet.

The first comprehensive assessment of the extinction, risk from global warming, found that more than one million species could be committed to extinction by 2050 if global warming pollution is not curtailed. This ranks global warming alongside direct habitat destruction as the greatest threat to global biodiversity. The nineteen-member research team featured expertise on ecosystems in five diverse regions: Mexico's Chihuahuan Desert; Amazonia; Europe; South Africa's Cape Floristic Region; and Queensland, Australia. The scientists used information on the climate tolerance of species and the well-known relationship between species' diversity and habitat area to project the effects of global warming under various assumptions. Their mid-range estimates indicate that 24 percent of existing species would eventually become extinct due to climate change project to occur by 2050." Fortunately, this risk could be significantly reduced by acting soon to reduce emissions of carbon dioxide and other heat-trapping gases according to the study.

Two American US government scientists, Dr. Thomas Karl of the National Atmospheric and Oceanic Administration and Dr. Kevin Trenberth of the National Center for Atmospheric Research, published a paper in the December 5, 2001, issue of Science, concluding that human influences are the dominant factor in recent global warming and that "in the absence of climate mitigation policies the likely result is more frequent heat waves, droughts, extreme precipitation events, and related impacts such as wildfires, heat stress, vegetation changes, and sea level rise."

The American Geophysical Union, the largest scientific organization of earth scientists, issued a new position statement on December 16, 2003, concluding that "scientific evidence strongly indicates that natural influences cannot explain the rapid increase in global near-surface temperatures observed during the second half of the twentieth century." The drafting committee for this consensus statement included John Christy, whose work to measure atmospheric temperatures using satellites is often cited by global warming naysayers.

The relatively small global warming that has occurred to date has already changed the habits or forced significant shifts in the range of many species of birds, insects, fish, and plants, according to the author of these two studies published in the prominent scientific journal *Nature*. "Such altered habits and forced moves from English butterflies, California starfishes, Estonian birds, and Alpine herbs could seriously disrupt a wide array of ecosystems." On the average, the species' geographic ranges have shifted toward the poles at a rate of 4 miles per decade and the species' spring events have shifted earlier by two days per decade. The data covered in the reports allowed the authors to express their findings with far greater certainty than they could have a decade ago.

The news is especially alarming considering such shifts have occurred with an average increase of only 1 degree Fahrenheit over the last century. If we are already seeing such a dramatic change among species, it is pretty frightening to think what we might see in the next one hundred years.

Scientists predict average global temperatures during the twenty-first century could jump as much as 10 degrees if we do not cut emissions of the heat-trapping gasses that cause global warming. The studies provide the latest compelling evidence that we must cut emissions of heat-trapping gasses like carbon dioxide to avoid widespread ecological disruption. They were conducted by researchers at Stanford, Wesleyan, and the University of Texas, among others.

Scientist say the dramatic disintegration of a Rhode Island-sized ice chunk off the Antarctic Peninsula in early 2002 is most likely the result of global warming. "With the disappearance of ice shelves that have existed for thousands of years, you rapidly run out of other explanations," Dr. Theodore A. Scambos, a glaciologist at the National Snow and Ice Data Center, told The New York Times after the Larsen B shelf collapsed. Scambos and other researchers said it was the first time in a thousand years that the east coast of Antarctica had seen such sharp rises in temperature and dramatic ice losses. Over the last fifty years, average temperatures in the Antarctica Peninsula have risen by 4.5 degrees Fahrenheit, four times the global average. The unprecedented warming has led to a pattern of ice shelves loss on the eastern side of the peninsula not seen in 12,000 years, researchers said. Scientists said they were also shocked by the speed with which the Larson B shelf disintegrated 1200 square miles in thirty-five days.

The National Climate Data Center and the World Meteorological Organization (WMO) also found the Earth's temperature for 2001 to be the second hottest on record. In addition, nine of the ten warmest years since measurements were first kept in 1860 have occurred since 1990. The WMO also found that temperatures are currently rising three times as fast as in the early twentieth century. The agency attributed much of the warming to heat-trapping gasses like carbon dioxide caused by the burning of fossil fuels. "There are skeptics on everything, but certainly the evidence we have today shows we do have global warming, and most of it is due to human action," Ken Davidson, the director of the WMO's climate program told The New York Times after the release of the report. The hottest year on record, according to the organizations, was 1998, when average global temperatures were 58.1 degrees Fahrenheit, average temperature for 2001 was 57.8 degrees according to the National Climatic Data Center.

A report from the National Academy of Science was requested by President Bush to determine whether mankind's actions were causing global warming. The answer was a resounding yes. The blue-ribbon panel found that "'greenhouse gasses are accumulating in the Earth's atmosphere as a result of human activities, causing surface air temperatures and subsurface ocean temperatures to rise." Temperatures are in fact rising, the report adds. The unanimous eleven-member panel, which included previous skeptics about global warming, said increasing temperatures posed a problem to humans and ecosystems around the globe. They also said the problem was getting worse. In addition, the panel stated that increased greenhouse gas concentrations were to blame for the Earth's 1 degree temperature increase over the past fifty years. Human-induced warming and associated sea level rise are expected to continue through the twenty-first century. National policy decision made now will influence the extent of the damage suffered by humans and ecosystems later this century.

The International Panel on Climate Change a United Nations sanctioned panel of hundreds of scientist released two landmark reports on climate change at the beginning of 2001. The first, known as the Working Group 1 report on the scientific basis of climate change, states unequivocally that pollution (mainly in the form of burning fossil fuels) causes climate change. "Emissions of greenhouse gases due to human activities continue to alter the atmosphere in ways that are expected to affect the climate." Global warming has caused sea levels to rise, ocean heat content to increase, and snow cover and ice extent to decrease. This and other evidences led the panel to conclude that there is new and stronger evidence that most of the warming experienced in the past fifty years is due to human activities. This report also predicts a 3 to 10 degree Fahrenheit rise in temperature during the twenty-first century. That increase would mark the most rapid change in ten millennia. It would also be as much as 60 percent higher than the IPCC predicted less than six years ago. The study found that warming in the twentieth century was the greatest of the last one thousand years and that the 1990s were the hottest decade of the last millennium.

The most profound report to date was ordered by congress, "Climate Change 2001: Impacts, Adaptation, and Vulnerability" is the most comprehensive look yet at the existing and long-term effects of global warming. It predicts that rising temperatures caused by the burning of fossil fuels could cause large-scale and irreversible climate changes. Those changes include altered ocean currents, slowed circulation of warm water in the North Atlantic, and a vast reduction of mountain glaciers and in the Greenland ice sheet. The study also warns of savage floods, disrupted water supplies, drought, violent storms, and the spread of cholera and malaria, as temperatures rise over the next century. Poor countries, particularly those in Latin America, Africa, and Asia, would bear most of the burden of extreme climate changes, which would further widen the gap between poor and rich nations. "Most of the Earth's people will be on the losing side" IPCC cochair and Harvard environmentalists' scientist James McCarthy said.

This study offers the first comprehensive assessment of how human-induced global warming will affect the United States. The forecast is gloomy; increasingly, there will be significant climate-related changes that will affect each one of us. The United States as the world's leading polluter per capita also will see a 5 to 10 degree Fahrenheit rise in temperature. This will cause the alpine meadows in the Rocky Mountains to disappear, sugar maple trees to vanish in the Northeast, and greater risk from storm surges in the Southeast. Rising temperatures will also exacerbate water shortages especially in the west. New York City will steam in the summer like Atlanta does now. Other likely impacts are the erosion of coastal states, destructive storm surges, and the disappearance of barrier islands due to the rise in the sea levels.

You might have heard the term "greenhouse effect" used when people refer to global warming, but what is the greenhouse effect?

A greenhouse is kept warm because energy coming in from the sun in the form of visible sunlight is able to pass through the glass and heats the soil and plants inside. But energy that is emitted from the soil and the plants in the form of invisible infrared radiation is not able to easily pass through the glass of the greenhouse. Some of the infrared heat energy is trapped inside. This is the main reason why a greenhouse is warmer inside than outside.

The atmosphere surrounding the Earth is made up of many different gasses. Some of these gasses such as carbon dioxide, methane nitrous oxide, and ozone act like a glass of a greenhouse. They let solar radiation or the energy from the sun pass through but prevent the exit of reflected radiation, thus, warming the Earth. Thus the "greenhouse effect."

The greenhouse effect keeps the Earth 21 degrees Celsius warmer than it would be otherwise.

The level of these gasses has remained relatively constant throughout the Earth's history. When levels have risen, for example, through volcanic activity, plant life has been able to increase in order to draw down the excess carbon dioxide from the atmosphere.

However, manufacturing processes used in industry and agriculture and the burning of fossil fuels have increased the amount of these gasses being released into the atmosphere.

Over the last two hundred years there has been a 40 percent increase in carbon dioxide concentrations.

This enhanced greenhouse effect means that the planet is gradually getting warmer and warmer.

There are many different effects of global warming, some of which seem unrelated to the small increases in temperature. The sun, apart from warming the Earth's surface, also causes the wind and the ocean waves. As the ground heats up, hot air rises and draws cold air down to replace it, creating wind. This evaporates water to give rainfall, and it powers photosynthesis in plants from which all life is derived.

We can separate the effects of global warming into three different categories: primary, secondary, and tertiary.

Primary—Apart from increases in extreme temperature, both hot and cold, we can expect to see major increases in wind force and wave heights with at least a 6 percent increase in storms and rainfall.

Secondary—As the oceans warm, seawater expands, icecaps melt, and the overall sea level will rise. The increase in wind and wave heights will pose severe threats to sea defenses. More rainfall will increase the threat of rivers bursting their banks and flooding will result.

Tertiary—Flooding, tidal waves, storms, and extreme temperatures will bring with them further problems. Destruction of property and crops will lead to increase in famines, disease epidemics, mass migration of populations, and an increase in major disasters. In order to combat these problems there will be an increased demand for energy.

How do we control global warming? The good news is that the solutions to the problem are clear. Most of our electricity comes from decades-old, dirty coal-burning power plants. These dinosaurs can be phased out and replaced with cleaner plants. Relying more on renewable energy sources, such as wind, solar power, and hydrogen fuel cells would drastically reduce global warming pollution.

California has required its largest utilities to get 20 percent of their electricity from renewable sources within fifteen years; other states could do the same. We can make our homes, offices, and industries much more energy-efficient, which would cut pollution and save money.

Each time you choose a compact fluorescent light bulb over an incandescent bulb, you will lower your electric bill and keep half a ton of carbon dioxide out of the air.

Hybrid gas-electric engines can cut global warming pollution by one third or more. Perhaps someday SUVs and mini vans will use this technology. Automakers have the technology right now to raise the fuel efficiency for cars and trucks to around 35 to 40 miles per gallon. By closing the loopholes and requiring SUVs, mini vans, and trucks to be as fuel efficient as cars would save 120 million tons of carbon dioxide a year.

By leaning more heavily on renewable energy sources such as wind, solar, and hydrogen fuel cells, we make an immediate impact on our environment.

We have the knowledge to make more efficient appliances to conserve energy at home, in the office, and on the road.

The United States has long been the world's leading developer of new technologies. However, we are also the leading global warming polluter with only 4 percent of the world's population. We produce 25 percent of the carbon dioxide pollution.

We have a responsibility as individuals and as a nation to lead the world toward slashing emissions of carbon dioxide and other heat-trapping gasses. We have the solutions to this problem, but we have to begin using them now.

Legacy of War

Radiation is inescapable, useful, and dangerous and understanding its benefits and risks is a necessary part of living in the atomic age.

While the word "radiation" is a broad term that includes sunlight and heat, it is most commonly used to refer to ionizing radiation, which is caused by the decay of atoms that releases energetic particles capable of damaging living cells. Humans have been aware of this kind of radiation for only a century.

Our bodies repair some radiation damage. Healthy cells fix themselves all the time. But massive doses of radiation can destroy cells, killing quickly, and milder doses can occasionally overcome the body's repairs and cause DNA damage that can trigger cancer or other diseases. This damage and repair cycle makes assessing the risk from nuclear waste, nuclear power plants, and fallout from nuclear testing extremely difficult. Scientist can predict with some accuracy that exposing many people to radiation will result is some percentage of them being harmed. They can't say whether low-level exposure will trigger cancer or other diseases in any individual.

Assessing radiation risk is further complicated because not all radiation is alike.

For example, alpha radiation is blocked by human skin, but gamma rays and neutrons are extremely penetrating.

Some radioactive isotopes are extremely dangerous in the short term but decay quickly and pose no long-term waste problem. The dangerous isotope of iodine, which may have caused thyroid disease among people living downwind from Hanford Washington in the

1940s and 1950s has a half-life of eight days and, thus, decays almost entirely in a few weeks.

Other isotopes persist a long time but give off weaker radiation. Plutonium, for example, has a half-life of 24,000 years but emits only alpha radiation. It is possible, though not advised, to hold a "button" of purified plutonium in one's hand without harm.

Plutonium is also unlikely to harm if swallowed. The body typically flushes it out of the digestive system before its weak radiation can have an effect. Plutonium is extremely dangerous if particles are breathed, however. They can lodge in the lungs and steadily give off radiation that could eventually trigger cancer.

Spent fuel from nuclear reactors is highly radioactive and hot. These long metal tubes are presently stored in water-filled pools next to nuclear-power plants, the water shielding the environment from the radiation. The tentative plan is to eventually package the fuel in dry casks and bury it underground, but the proposed depository at Yucca Mountain in Nevada may be abandoned by Congress.

Transuranic waste is less radioactive waste that comes chiefly from fuel reprocessing or weapons production and has a half-life of twenty years or more. There are half a million drums of this stored in warehouses and dirt pads around the United States. An underground salt mine in Carlsbad, New Mexico, called the waste Isolation Pilot Plant, has been prepared to accept this waste but has not yet been approved for operation. New Mexico opposes its opening.

Low-level waste differs from transuranic waste in that it has a shorter half-life. It comes from power plants, hospitals, laboratories, factories, and so on. It is typically sealed in drums and buried at specific landfills, including the one at Hanford.

There are about 8,700 radioactive and chemically contaminated sites in the United States that the Department of Energy is responsible for cleaning up. The agency also hopes to clean and demolish 20,000 buildings on its 2.3 million acres no-longer-needed-for-bomb manufacturing.

When the Cold War ended, America's nuclear warhead production system shut down so rapidly that weapons-grade isotopes were left stranded, so to speak, on the assembly line.

A WINNING BUSINESS

The United States had produced one hundred finished tons of plutonium from which to fashion warheads. Fifty-three of those tons were made at Hanford, Washington (1942–present), the oldest and perhaps largest nuclear waste storage facility. Another twenty-six tons were in intermediate steps before weapons fabrication.

Dealing with these leftovers has become one of the top cleanup priorities at the Hanford site in Eastern Washington. The Seattle Times recently got a rare peek at the plutonium storage vaults there encased in a windowless concrete building and locked behind five thousand-pound doors.

Hanford's Plutonium Finishing Plant is the factory where liquid nitrate solutions of plutonium from the nuclear reservation's Purex Plant were turned into palm-sized silvery "buttons" that could be machined into warheads.

Each button cost $2.8 million to produce, and the laborious process of going from liquid to solid metal took about two weeks. Technicians used soft gold drills to probe the button interiors, testing for quality.

Abrupt shutdown left a residue of plutonium and chemicals along the gritty conveyer line. Now workers are carefully scraping off the gunk, heating it in small ovens to 1,000 degrees Celsius to bum off potentially explosive gasses and reduce its volume, and then packing it in led-lined cans, one inside another. They look like large food cans.

If all this waste were stacked together, the concentrated radioactivity could spark a chain reaction and a fire or meltdown. Accordingly, the cans are taken to the plutonium storage vault and stored inside lockers.

Hanford is probably most notorious for that of a "tank farm." Sixty-one million gallons of nuclear and chemical waste is held in storage facilities, some fifty years old and leaking.

There are speculations that the chemicals from Hanford are to blame for the massive multiple sclerosis population in the Pacific Northwest. There are statistics that discuss how many people have contracted multiple sclerosis that have lived in the region their entire lives. Although there is no specific data to prove the cause is due to

Hanford, it is hard not to question that such a chemical "tank farm" could be the culprit.

These tanks will remain in Hanford for the foreseeable future. While the plutonium and nuclear waste will persist for tens of thousands of years, no decision has been made about its long-term fate. The plutonium could be turned into glass and buried or refabricated into reactor fuel.

The storage vault holding plutonium is monitored by the International Atomic Energy Agency, the same United Nations body that polices Iraq. The product can't be moved without them knowing about it.

The history of the Rocky Flats (1952–1990) facility in Denver, Colorado, sparked widespread fear and panic throughout the region.

Armed with a search warrant, the FBI seized thousands of documents from the plant on allegations they had illegally dumped toxic waste into drinking water sources and had operated an incinerator that had been closed for safety reasons.

After all the testimony, on March 26, 1992, the US attorney Michael Norton announced that Rockwell International, the company that had been operating the nuclear weapons plant for fourteen years, had pleaded guilty to ten charges of violating federal hazardous waste disposal and clean water laws. The US attorney, recommending an $18.5 million fine, Rockwell executives had agreed to pay. In one of the most celebrated criminal cases of environmental misconduct in the country's history, only court approval of the settlement and fine remained.

Those who had been following the case at Rocky Flats were stunned. Federal agents had spent more than three years investigating allegations of serious violations at the plant. A grand jury, seated for two and a half years, had heard testimony from 110 witnesses and examined 760 boxes of documents.

So why was Rockwell's fine smaller than the government's bonuses it won while operating the plant? Why didn't the grand jury, after all its work, not return a single indictment against anyone, including the executives making decisions? Why were individ-

A WINNING BUSINESS

ual Rockwell employees and their supervisors at the Department of Energy not going to be held accountable?

Norton noted the fine would be the largest ever collected by the federal government for violations of hazardous waste disposal laws, but he would not comment on the actions of the grand jury. In accordance with federal law, he said, "Those were and would remain secret."

Every step in the process of manufacturing nuclear weapons produces radioactive and chemical waste. For every pound of plutonium that is produced, 170 gallons of high-level waste and 27,000 gallons of low-level waste is produced. This has resulted in enough waste to completely fill a 1,000-foot supertanker. Most of this waste is being stored in two locations: Savannah River, South Carolina, and Hanford, Washington.

The fear of nuclear and chemical waste has caused most of the states to fight Congress against having it buried in their backyard. The cleanup of these sights will take decades, maybe longer. With all the technology today, there must be a way to destroy these chemicals without letting them seep into our environment These radioactive isotopes and chemical wastes have effected tens of thousands of people since the first nuclear bomb was created. The question is how much longer will this go on.

About the Author

A business executive with a history of success specializing in real estate sales, marketing, and new business development. Particularly skilled at daily oversight for a custom home business and extensive knowledge in real estate sales, development, and construction. Background includes licensed insurance agent, licensed real estate agent, sales executive for independent real estate development company, and president of a custom home company.

A keen ability to influence sales force by example, motivation, innovation, and personal drive. Consistent focus on identifying opportunities for revenue development with new and existing customers. Skilled at conveying honesty and integrity to lead a management team.

www.ingramcontent.com/pod-product-compliance
Lightning Source LLC
Chambersburg PA
CBHW022113170526
45157CB00004B/1609